THE GOSPEL
ACCORDING TO
MALFEW SEKLEW

The
GOSPEL
According To
MALFEW
SEKLEW
and other writings by and about
SIRFESSOR
WILKESBARRE
with an introduction by
TREVOR BLAKE

UNDERWORLD AMUSEMENTS
BALTIMORE

ISBN: 978-0-9885536-8-2

Paperback edition published by Underworld Amusements.
UnderworldAmusements.com

If you have information about or writings by Malfew Seklew that you don't see represented here, please contact us.

Contents

Entrance to the Dil Pickle Club of Chicago, circa 1927.

There is Only One Malfew Seklew and Sirfessor Wilkesbarre is His Prophet

I
Biography of a Supercrat

Fred Wilkes was born in England in the 1860s. For his bread he lived by his wits. He sold clip-on ties as a street vendor in Manchester and briefly held an herb and sausage shop in Nottingham. But he achieved enlightenment and renown as a street orator and master of public debate.

The experience enriched his already expansive ego. Wilkes granted himself the title of Sirfessor, one step above a Professor. Thus ennobled he took on a multitude of monikers. Fredrick Wilkesbarre, Mr. Wilkes Barre, Sirfessor F. W. Barre, F. Wilkes-Barre, the Laughing Philosopher of Lancashire, his life too full to be contained in a single name. And one new name above all others rings across a century to turn our heads: Malfew Seklew. There is a fine literary tradition of quoting another to give one's own ideas more weight, and should no other be worthy of one's own weight then an invented identity is ideal. There is no Superman without Clark Kent, no Zorro without Don Diego de la Vega, and I decline to say Sirfessor Wilkesbarre "was" Malfew Seklew. Egoism values the self above all, and it makes sense to have several selves. The Sirfessor sometimes spoke for himself, but often would play the straight man to Seklew.

Sirfessor Wilkesbarre penned a number of pointed pamphlets against politicians while in the UK. His first literary work of length was as co-editor of *The Eagle and The Serpent*, a funny little egoist journal in every sense from the late 1890s. Here the Sirfessor rubbed egoist elbows with contemporary contrarians such as Jim Tully and E. Haldeman-Julius. Among the more famous names to appear in the letter section of *The Eagle and The Serpent* were psychic investigator Hereward Carrington, eugenicist Albert Wiggam, author George Bernard Shaw and anarchist Peter Kropotkin.

Sirfessor Wilkesbarre came to the United States in his 50s in 1916. At the dawn of the Twentieth Century, Sirfessor Wilkesbarre was a regular at the contrarian hobo college known as the Dil Pickle Club in Chicago, Illinois. So was Ragnar Redbeard, and in fact the two shared 1353 North Clark Street (at least as a mailing address) in 1927. That same year the Dil Pickle Club published Redbeard's *Might is Right* and Wilkesbarre published *The Gospel According to Malfew Seklew*. I imagine that Condo and Raper, the author and artist for the contemporary Chicago comic *The Outbursts of Everett True*, concocted central character Mr. True on Wilkesbarre's looks and Redbeard's thunder. Also in Chicago the Sirfessor was a regular contributor and subject in local newspapers (a primitive form of internet, for you youngsters) such as *The Day Book*.

Illustration of Sirfessor Wilkesbarre by Alex Rosenfeld that accompanied the article "Worlds Remade, While You Wait—On the East Side" from the New-York Tribune *of Jan. 26, 1919.*

A man who lives with little punching of the time-clock is still measured in his days. The culture of street debate of 1890s England found a small analog in the hobo colleges of 1920s Chicago, but no one was hiring the happily homeless in 1930s New York City. Sirfessor Wilkesbarre's story in New York is one of loss. Radio interviews that were never recorded, lost competitions for non-stop talking, lost book manuscripts, loss of corpulence and in time the loss of his lividly lived life.

II
Selfishness is the Eternal Energy
Seeking Expression Through Mankind

While conversant in both the English and American languages, he did not favour the spelling of either civilization. Sirfessor Wilkesbarre was largely at liberty from labor. He therefore had the time to become self-educated, a master mind manufactured to order. When you don't work for a living, you have time to read. And read, and read, and read. Thus *The Gospel According To Malfew Seklew* is aquiver with quotations. As might be expected, in *The Gospel* I find references to fellow egoists such as Max Stirner, Tak Kak, E. D. Linton, Morse Monroe, John Erwin McCall and Ragnar Redbeard. Other outsiders are here included, such as anarchist Josiah Warren and atheist John William Gott, cartoonist Don Marquis and hobo poet A. W. Dragstedt. In *The Gospel* there are leaders like Napoleon Bonaparte, Lord Balfour, Richard Haldane, Benjamin Disraeli, Charles Summer and Abraham Lincoln. To one side we find occultists, Rosicrucians, Theosophics, psychics and spiritual utopians. To the other we find Jesus Christ, Buddha, Brahma, Mohammed, Lao Tzu, and Swami Saraswati. The good Sirfessor is able to cite philosophers such as Nietzsche, Socrates, Heraclitus, Hume, Spencer, Schopenhauer, Descartes, Protagoras, Hippocrates, Marx, Publius, Schiller, Rousseau, Emerson, Pythagoras, Marcus Aurelius, Comte, Hobbes and Paine. Scientists of the mind such as Sigmund Freud, Wilhelm Stekel, Lester Frank Ward, Gustave Le Bon, and William James are found here. Found here also are scientists of the world such as Herbert Spencer, Charles Darwin, Isaac Newton and Gregor Mendel. Contemporaries include the equally self-taught author Will Durant and

Sample page from Change for a Half-Penny, *published in London, 1905.*

the aviator Charles Lindbergh (whose transoceanic flight happened only months before *The Gospel* was published). And for all the high-brow reading, Sirfessor Wilkesbarre was also able to cite with delight musicals by Gilbert & Sullivan and the college boy's humor book *Change for a Halfpenny*. More than anything else, Sirfessor Wilkesbarre quotes from literature. Here we see poets and playwrights, authors and diarists. Alphabetically, then... Austin, Bierce, Blake, Butler, de Cervantes, Chamfort, Chesterton, Cowper, Dickinson, Goethe, Hugo, Ibsen, Ingalls, Ingelow, Johnson, Kipling, de Mandeville, Martial, de Montaigne, Plutarch, La Rochefoucauld, Ruffini, Shakespeare, Shaw, Shelley, Stevenson, Swift, Tennyson, Voltaire, Walpole, Wilde and Wollstonecraft. Not to mention that most celebrated of authors, anon.

The Gospel According to Malfew Seklew in part takes the form of egoist sutras, numbered lists of forbidden and compulsory actions dictated by a master without slaves to a concentrated corps of contrarians who will, of course, do what we will anyway.

When the body hungers, it is to be filled with food. When a book hungers, it is to be filled with writing about food. Seemingly a foreign body lodged in the throat of *The Gospel of Malfew Seklew*, right in the middle we find a lengthy feast from the nutrition writings of Josiah Reddie Mallet. Think of it as filler to plump out what might have been a more paltry pamphlet, or as the delicious bait that could appeal to many hiding a hook to catch the egoist few, or as egoism applied in the maintenance of the Self. Think of it as *Ecce Homo*, or not at all. The Sirfessor quoted it, Mr. Slaughter published it and that settles it.

The eternally exalted exit wound erupting from the body politic is *The Ego and Its Own* by Max Stirner (1844). Nietzsche is the name of note among supporters of the superman, but attend to this quote from *The Ruin of Kasch* by Roberto Calasso in which Ida Overbeck (wife of Freddy's friend Franz Overbeck) pulls the crib-notes from the master's sleeve:

> Once, when my husband was out, Nietzsche stayed and talked to me for a while, telling me about two strange characters he was dealing with at the time—people with whom he felt a kinship. As is always the case when one finds some internal rapport, he was animated and happy. Some time later he found a book by Klinger in our house. My husband had not found Stirner in the library. 'Ah,' said Nietzsche, 'I was mistaken about Klinger. He was a Philistine: I feel no affinity at all with him. But Stirner—with him, yes.' A grave expression darkened his face. And as I looked attentively at his features, they changed again. He waved his hand, as if to drive away or repel something, and murmured: 'Now I've told you, and I didn't want to speak of it. Forget it all. They will talk of plagiarism, but I know you won't.'

The Ego and Its Own is light—a beam of light, and the light of laughter and laviciousness. It is a delight to read and looks like the author was having fun as he wrote it. A fine wellspring for egoism, and one I sought to draw from in my own *Confessions of a Failed Egoist*. Dora Marsden pursued an intellectual egoism all the way to the mental hospital, and Ragnar Redbeard shouted the blood and thunder of might is right. I love them all, but they don't all make me laugh. For that I turn to Stirner and to Seklew. Not every jot and tittle will jolt a titter, but the laugh track record is Olympic. Sirfessor Wilkesbarre is a winking star in the egoist heavens.

What literacy was to the ancient world and what industrialization was to yesterday's world, artificial intelligence is to tomorrow. It is the universal solvent that dissolves all that is not itself. Whether you want to promote or prohibit AI, the philosophy of the individual—egoism—is the only ethics equipped to explain the imminent extropian eschaton. Note the Sirfessor's promise as a prophet. A good half century before young Richard Dawkins wrote of the selfish gene, our hero argued against altruism as a fundamental principle of nature: "Certain men, who have had the courage to probe down to the very bottom of their own minds, have come to the conclusion that self-interest is the only motive of all human action: i might say of all action that is not merely mechanical and has life at the root of it... What is life? Just one thing after another." Fifty years further we find Our Bill said Wilkesbarre "rips the mask of sham and pretense from the hypocrites and fakers and will be appreciated about 100 years after he is dead." And from the Sirfessor himself: "If you wish to live 100 years begin today to laugh." Right on schedule, an onus is upon us for egoist evangelism glorifying *The Gospels*.

Trevor Blake
Portland, Oregon
August 2014

Panel from The Outbursts of Everett True, *circa 1920.*

Richard G. McKnight, Individualist Anarchist, (left)
with Sirfessor Wilkesbarre (right).

Editor's Note

The Gospel According to Malfew Seklew and Other Writings By and About Sirfessor Wilkesbarre is divided into a four distinct sections: the front matter, the *Gospel* book as it was published in 1927, "The Day Book Debates," and "Bellows and Recollections."

Through the book we have made a few sparse footnotes. We have tried to add clarification on forgotten historical references, reattributed interesting quotations where they lacked it, and produced other clarifications where we thought would be useful to the reader. The original had none, so all here are by myself or Mr. Blake. When possible we tried to list the most probable source of the quotation given the date and other attributes.

Because many people are quoted multiple times through the book, the first instance will feature full name (or real name, in many cases), birth and death years, and what they were known for. Subsequent footnoted attributions by the same person will eschew this biographical information for brevity, only noting source and any additional notes.

The Gospel

Two publications were printed with the title *The Gospel According to Malfew Seklew*. The first is a pamphlet containing the essay "Egoism: Conscious and Unconcious," as well as two other longer essays, "The Man Without a Soul" and "The Invention of God," and some other miscellaneous material. This was a promotional item, and certainly printed by the same people who produced pamphlets for Ragnar Redbeard. Mr. Blake and

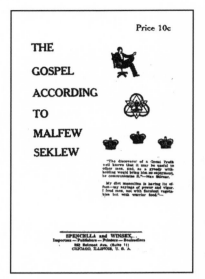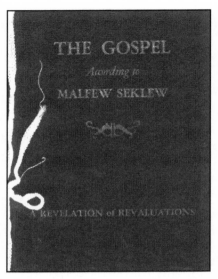

A pamphlet teaser (left), and the first edition of the book (right).

I agree that some of the material and at least one of the essays from the pamphlet was co-written with Ragnar Redbeard. As Mr. Blake has noted, the two of them worked together on other projects, and shared a mailing address. Both "Egoism" and "The Invention of God" are signed "Sirfessor Superight," possibly an intentional variant of Wilkesbarre's pen name "Sirfessor Superite",[001] by making reference to Redbeard's *magnum opus Might is Right*.

While we believe "Egoism" is probably largely (or entirely) written by Wilkesbarre, and it appears in the book version of *Gospel* without modified attribution, "The Invention of God" lacks much of Wilkesbarre's trademark writing quirks and style, and we conclude that it was largely (or entirely) written by Redbeard, whose writings it most reflects. Further proof of collaboration on the piece is its inclusion in a pamphlet of quotations by Ragnar Redbeard. Because of these and other reasons we have decided to leave it out of our book, though it will be reprinted in a collection of "lost" writings of Redbeard to be published by Underworld Amusements.

---

001   Mr. Blake has written a short history of the use of "multiple names" in his book *Confessions of a Failed Egoist*.

The other selections have been reprinted in the last section of this book, titled "Bellows and Recollections."

The first edition of *Gospel* has a gold-stamped, black card cover and ribbon binding. Our edition reproduces his entire text with much improved typography. Malfew Seklew's *Gospel* is an odd book. Not just in the sense that he was a radical of his time, advocating and then ultimately rejecting the Socialism and Anarchism of his fellow radicals and subsequently preaching a pro-capitalist Nieztschean Individualism, but in the sense it's also a rather disjointed collection of short essays, quotes, epigrams, lists and more lists, and even a section on dietary recommendations. It also fails to retain a consistent flow in how the material is presented. In this sense, it is a wonderful representation of "crank" literature.

The Day Book Debates

This section includes 33 letters written to the Chicago-based daily newspaper *The Day Book* (1911-1917). The newspaper was an experiment, as it was free of advertising and specifically targeted toward the working class—the publisher referred to his audience as "the 95 percent." Though many of the letters here were written by Wilkesbarre, we have included others that comment on him and his writing. The result is a sort of conversation allowing for a greater context to his words, and also represent some of the response during the time they were written.

Bellows & Recollections

This section is a mix of writings by and about Wilkesbarre/Seklew in his various guises. The first essay. "J. Bruce Glasier: Demi-Gods Demi-Damned..." was a sketch of the Scottish Socialist politician (25 March 1859 - 4 June 1920) published as a booklet in 1906 by John W. Gott.

"Politics and Parliament," "A Napoleon of Labor" and "The

Wit, Wisdom and Wickedness of Malfew Seklew" are sourced from the aforementioned *Gospel* pamphlet. In the pamphlet "Politics and Parliament" is signed "The Man Without a Soul" and "A Napoleon of Labor" is signed "A Brutalitarian Truthist."

"An Answer to a Symposium" is pulled from an issue of *The Eagle and The Serpent*. A regular feature was to get numerous people to respond to a set of questions or statements. Other contributors to the symposium were: Robert Washington, Upton Sinclair, Joseph Peterson, John B. Watson, E. Haldeman-Julius, Albert Schinz, Jim Tully, Hereward Carrington, A. E. Wiggam, Stanley Walker.[002] For this, he signed "F.M. Wilkesbarr."

The bullet-point like comparison "Individualism and Socialism" was found in the same issue as the "Symposium."

The three following parts are all "recollections," excerpts dealing with Seklew/Wilkesbarre from larger works.

"The Noun and Verb Rodeo" documents Wilkesbarres involvement in a "talking marathon," covered fairly widely in his day.

In "Malfew Seklew Solves All Problems of Life" Mr. Blake has collected from numerous publications a list of lecturing and speaking engagements. Certainly, since Wilkesbarre was known to stand on soap-boxes in city squares, it would be impossible to compile a full list of public speaking, however this does provide a glimpse into some of the topics and locations where he was to be found.

The book finishes with two obituaries, followed by an advertisement and description of one Wilkesbarre's few known modes of income, selling the Superite Tie-Frame.

Kevin I. Slaughter
Baltimore, Maryland
August, 2014

---

002   The book *A Bible Not Borrowed from the Neighbors, Essays and Aphorisms on Egoism* reprints many essays and quotations originally printed in *The Eagle and The Serpent*.

The GOSPEL *According To* MALFEW SEKLEW

A Bible for Supercrats and Egocrats

A Religion of Reality for Realism and Idealists

A Testament for Creative Evolutionists

The Secret of Salvation Revealed

Salvation for All and One

1927

Not to succumb to the unchangeable forces of Nature, but to direct them; not to allow ourselves to be enslaved by them, but to make use of them to the benefit of (humanity) immortal liberty; this is the great secret of life.

—Eliphas Levi.

It is the age of wonder; of the marvelous inventions of men there is no end. But who will invent a way of making plain truth known to all men?

"The discoverer of a Great Truth well knows that it may be useful to other men, and, as a greedy withholding would bring him no enjoyment, he communicates it."

—Max Stirner.[001]

---

001   Max Stirner (1806 - 1856). Philosopher, father of Egoism. Quote from *The Ego and Its Own*.

Malfew Seklew for many years wandered up and down Great Britain, preaching unto mankind his philosophy of Enlightened Egoism.

The writings herein published are but fragments. And yet they are complete. Each thought is a thought at itself. With one idea left out, the whole would not be whole, but unfinished, incomplete.

They were chosen and compiled because they are representative of the thought of the man and his philosophy.

Wrested as they are from their settings, they remain nevertheless—gems.

Men are born only to die. A few, however, leave their footprints in the sands of Time. We are able to guide ourselves by them.

The Gospel According to Malfew Seklew is for the individual who is seeking for footprints that he might be so guided.

If they cause one to think a bit, if they tend to make one see life a bit clearer, they have not been compiled in vain.

PREFACE

For ages man has been chasing rainbows and following false gods, without any good results.

Prophets, Messiahs and Redeemers have had their day and gone their way, leaving little behind to benefit mankind: Jesus, St. Paul, Buddha, Brahma, Confucius, Mohammet—all have been tried and found wanting in driving sin, suffering, poverty, and ignorance from the world.

Man has been worshipping gods afar, unaware of the fact that the great God of humanity is contained within himself. When man has found this God he can emancipate himself from all that he considers evil. The Kingdom of Heaven is within you:

> "Seek first the Kingdom of Knowledge and Wisdom, and all things shall be added unto you, even the peace that passeth all misunderstanding."
>
> —Malfew Seklew.

Man can be his own god when he has found himself out, from within. Man can make his own heaven and his own hell after he has been born again and has become an Enlightened Egoist, or Ego Conscious organism.

Read, mark, learn, and inwardly digest this impression of the march of men from Nebulosity to Knowledge; from an Ego in the Crude to a Superman[002] in the Nude; and Victory is yours, crowned with Self Consciousness.

---

002   See *Thus Spake Zarathustra* by Friedrich Nietzche.

Quotations

"Only when man shall know himself, shall he know all things."

"The one purpose of every sane human being is to be happy. No one can have any other motive than that. There is no such thing as unselfishness. We perform the most 'generous' and 'self-sacrificing' acts because we should be unhappy if we did not. What increase the beggarly sum of human happiness is worth having; nothing else has any value."
—Ambrose Bierce. [003]

"Search mankind from pole to pole / You'll find self-interest guides them all."

"For all seek their own."
—Phil. 2:21. [004]

"Character is what we are in the dark."

"Through interest alone we condemn vice, and extol virtue. Interest blinds some people and enlightens others."
—La R. [005]

Montaigne[006] says: "Though we are all equally men, all men are not equal."

"There was only one good, namely, knowledge; and only one evil, namely, ignorance."
—Socrates.

---

003   Ambrose Bierce (1842 - c1914). Quote from: *A Cynic Looks at Life*.
004   "For all seek their own, not the things which are Jesus Christ's." - Philippians 2:21
005   François de La Rochefoucauld (1613 - 1680). Author, *Reflections; or Sentences and Moral Maxims*.
006   Michel de Montaigne (1533 - 1592). Author, *Essais*.

"Philosophy it seems is no more than an interpretation of the universe in terms of consciousness."

—*New Age.* [007]

"Mental processes are essentially unconscious, and those which are conscious are merely isolated acts and parts of the whole psychic entity."

—Prof. Freud. [008]

"Though the changing circumstances and impressions
        that we find,
Are largely in the Nature of a personal state of mind,
This world is like a mirror where reflected moods we see,
The way you think about it is the way it's going to be."

---

007   *New Age,* a periodical also cited by egoist Dora Marsden.
008   Sigmund Freud (1856 - 1939). Founder, psychoanalytic psychology.

Selfishness or Selfism.
Supercratic Egoism or Enlightened Selfullness.

"There is something chaotic, yet complete, that existed before man, and is now the dominating factor in the lives
of all human beings. Oh, how still it is, and how formless,
and yet how powerful! Standing alone without changing,
reaching everywhere without suffering harm, it is a great
square with no angles. It is a great image with no form."

It is a great voice that cannot be heard except by a few Unique
Egos. It has the power of transmuting and perfecting all things.

This Mighty Magician, this miracle of mind and matter, has
many labels. Some call it the Great Transformer, the Cosmic
Urge, the Great Spirit, the Eternal Energy, Vital Force, others
call it God. The Truthseeker calls it Selfishness. Selfishness has
all the attributes of the Godhead. It is Omnipotent, Omni-
scient, and Omnipresent. It is the parent of passion, prejudice,
pride, and all the vices; and the progenitor of faith, fortune, and
all the virtues to be found in mankind. It is Nature's masterpiece for good or evil.

This great principle of pain and pleasure can not be denied
without injury to self.

Nature produced Unity: Selfishness. Unity produced Duality: Self Love, which never dies; and self-interest, which rules
the world. Duality produced Trinity: Love, Vanity, and Hate;
and this trinity tantalizes, torments and tortures mankind, until the Ego Conscious organism becomes the Captain of his
own Ego and the Director of his own Destiny.

All these dynamic forces are the offspring of selfishness.

They are the Eternal Verities that govern our lives, and the
Everlasting Virtues that rule mankind, for good or evil. As a

philosopher wisely said:

> "Selfishness is at once my most essential friend, and my most dangerous enemy, for it is the zenith and nadir of desire, and the alpha and omega of aspiration."

The highest purpose of intellectual cultivation is to give man a perfect knowledge and mastery of his inner self. To attain this knowledge one must study the philosophy of Scientific Egoism, which examines and explains the motives, emotions, passions, prejudices and desires of the Ego; with the result that we find that all these dynamic forces are regulated by the Magic Power of Selfishness, for Selfishness is the Eternal Energy seeking expression through mankind, thus enabling man to find himself out, from within.

Selfishness is essential, absolute, changeless, and everlasting.

Selfishness is the Infinite Force that controls all life, especially human life. Selfishness is responsible for all the evil in the world, as well as for all the good. Man catering to his passions brings on pain; man catering to his desires brings on disease; man catering to his ignorance brings on poverty, and sins against himself. This is man unconscious of his own Ego, of his own necessities, of his real needs, and of his own powers. Ego Conscious Man, aware of his possibilities, realizes that the same force that brought misery and pain will, when understood, bring pleasure and power—to one and all.

• • •

All Life is selfish; all Reform is selfish; all Politics is selfish; all War is selfish; all Business is selfish; all Thought is selfish; all Action is selfish; All is selfish, and selfishness is rampant with and without reason throughout the world.

Selfishness is necessary to preserve one's self;

Vanity is necessary to assert one's self;

And hate is necessary to protect one's self from one's enemies.

Even Mother love is a very selfish love. Biologically and instinctively a mother does her best for her offspring; but psychologically she is the unconscious enemy of her child. She transfers all her delusions, prejudices, and superstitions to her children, if she is ignorant and uneducated. Just as readily does she transfer her wisdom, tolerance, and kindliness when she is progressive and cultured. In both cases she does it to satisfy herself. The results, however, are different.

An ignorant mother perpetuates her ignorance from one generation to another, thus impeding progress. Such mothers are the enemies of evolution, and the matrix of mediocrities.

The mother of the genius is an exception, because she is psychologically great. Genius is a psychological conception, rather than a biological production. Ignorant mothers produce inferior organisms. That is the reason why mediocrity is the malady of the day. The wise mother moulds the child during the period of gestation into the design she has in her mind. Every great man is the special product of such a mother.

When woman becomes aware of her psychological powers, miraculous perceptions will be as plentiful as commonplace conceptions are today. The genius-to-order will be the order of the day. Poets, artists, writers, scientists, and aristocrats of all kinds will be as plentiful as cheap organisms are nowadays. Enlightened Selfishness will demand the best and get it. Mind will mould matter to its own design. Will the Fulcrum of Fancy, and the Director of Desire, will regulate the Destiny of the super-child to be.

Woman as the Monarchess of Mentality will become the Chemist of Consciousness; the Alchemist of Humanity; and the Originator of Supermanity.

• • •

Love based on ignorance is like unbridled selfishness, a calamity and a curse to all that come in contact with its force. Love sanitized by reason, and selfishness enlightened by experiments and experience, will eradicate ignorance in time; and make wisdom welcome for all time.

Love is selfishness satisfied for a short time. It is the propagation of passion, or passion in pain, striving for peace again.

• • •

Why does evil exist in the world? Because everyone is born ignorant, and very few of mankind escape from this curse until they are old enough to die. Before the Enlightened Ego can transfer his wisdom to his fellow men in sufficient numbers to dominate the prevailing ignorance, a new generation of ignorant Egos comes upon the scene to swamp the effort of the reformers and to perpetuate the conditions where ignorance is ever in the ascendant.

• • •

All so-called acts of self-denial are really attempts to attain self-realization. To live up to one's own standard of morality, or code of honor, is the aim of the Ego; regardless of the fact that such action is founded on a selfish basis. His motive is self-approval.

• • •

Character is moulded by external and internal impressions. From without, we are pounded by events and by our clashes with our environment; from within, our thoughts are largely guided by what we read and imagine.

• • •

"I use the term Egoism, like Stirner, for acts of normal self-possession and self-expression, excluding blind crazes, fanaticism, the influence of fixed ideas, hypnotism dominating the subject and rendering him more of an automaton than an individual, although he goes through the motions. Rewards and punishments, promised and threatened, appeal to the Egoism of ignorant believers, but there is also an anti-individualistic craze or fascination in religion, and love and business, when the idea rides the man. In the last analysis it is a question of sanity or insanity."[009]

Egoism is sanity. Egoism is not merely an idea; it is as fact, the force of a man untrammeled by superstition. It may be more or less generous or ungenerous; thus it may be called selfish or unselfish in common speech. He may be more or less impulsive, more or less deliberate and reflecting. He may so feel and act as to be called very dutiful; but the Egoist relation to all objects is conditioned quite differently from that of the mentally unfree man. If he cares for others it is not because he is taught that it is his "duty"—a teaching that would make restraint out of an attraction; but it is because he is built that way, and this he knows.

Selfishness governs, alike, the good and the bad individual; the wise and the wicked Ego. The good Ego may do a kind act to another; the bad individual may do an unkind act to his brother. Both work from the same motive, self-gratification, with different results. The first is noble, because it is founded on wisdom; the second is ignoble, because it is founded on ignorance. The first is the source of all good; the second the source of all evil. The first brings concord; the second stirs up discord. The first is the conduct of an enlightened Egoist; the second is the action of an ignorant Egotist. Ignorance is the great Sin; Wisdom is the only salvation from sin and evil. The secret of salvation revealed for one and all. Choose for yourself.

• • •

There is no crime recognized by us as such which has not somewhere and at some time been found and recognized as a virtue, and no virtue which has not been officially condemned. The murderous Fijians only fear is lest he should not be active enough in slaughter to win the approbation of his gods; with the Egyptians lying is honorable; while the Turkoman's code of moral injunctions prescribe theft. Polygamy is wrong in Europe

009   Written by Tak Kak in a letter to the Editor of the journal *Liberty*. Vol. V, No. 7, March 31, 1888.

and America, but right and proper in China, India and Turkey. While infanticide, a practice we hold in abhorrence, is practiced in China and India without any qualms of conscience.

Science now tells us that not only is every particle of matter, or every mass of matter, in a state of continual vibration, but also that light, heat, magnetism, electricity and every other form of Natural force results from a state of vibration.

In fact the distinction between the several planes of being is almost entirely due to the difference in the rate and character of the vibrations manifested. The difference between gold and steel, or diamond and clay, is entirely a matter of difference in vibrations. The conditions of material substances are created by the respective degree of vibrations manifested by each. In like manner the difference in men is the degree of in Ego Consciousness. The man of enlightened understanding and persevering ardor has many sources of enjoyment which the ignorant man cannot reach.

$$\bullet \bullet \bullet$$

Infinite powers are slumbering undeveloped and unused in the bosom of a nation. In the mind of thousands and thousands of men there is genius hidden which is trying vainly to soar because poverty and lowliness paralyze it. While a country may be waining in weakness and pining for a great man, perhaps in a miserable hut a Caesar may be following the plow or a Lincoln chopping logs.

Man unconscious of his own possibilities hitherto has been the slave of his tools of production, and therefore the of circumstances. The Ego Conscious man changes his tools as he changes his mind. Then he changes his tastes and manages the future according to his tastes and manages the future according to his present consciousness.

It seems to me to be like this: weak men are the creatures of circumstances, but circumstances are the creatures of Man.

Conscience, the humanities, and religious emotions, all are enemies of mankind unless resting on a foundation of egoistic consciousness. Christian ethics, moral or altruistic behavior, to be
of any permanent value must be rooted in Egoistic wisdom. The
reason that Christian morality has no lasting value is because
it is founded on the false assumption that man is, Naturally, a
moral, a social, and a religious animal. The fact is, man becomes
moral and social from selfish reasons. Experience teaches man
that enlightened Egoism is the force for good in this world of
false formulas and stale shibboleths.

•••

Did you ever hear a man say: "There are no strings on me"—and
yet we know there are strings on all of us. Strings of fear, strings
of self-interest, strings of envy, strings of false pride, strings of
vanity: All these strings move people and together they pull
people to what they call their fate.

As soon as men know the nearest, cheapest and best way to
improve their lot, either morally, intellectually, or financially,
they will accept it with thankfulness if they have the opportunity and the power.

All we need to abolish crime, misery, poverty, and ignorance
is to purify our prejudices by learning how to socialize our selfishness. To be truly happy each Ego must have a chance to develop his own individuality, which is only another way of saying
each one must have the power to be selfish with his or her own
peculiar way.

•••

Selfishness is the life impetus which overlooks the good—and
yet can overcome evil when properly understood.

•••

The highest law of mind is Self Consciousness. Consciousness
consists of knowing how to do the right thing at the right time,

so as to bring desirable results by using the experience of the past for the benefit of the present and for the future good.

• • •

The Social Supercrat finds pleasure in doing things that brings pleasure to himself and others, because the more pleasure he procures, the more happiness he secures. The halo of happiness may be worn by all thinkers.

The gospel of Enlightened Selfishness—or Egoistic Self-full-ness—must be preached before malignant selfishness can he de-throned; and benevolent selfishness can be crowned with the Crest of the Conqueror, and the Wreaths of the Righteous. It will pay in every way to be an Enlightened Egoist, because it is Nature's only way to Cosmic Consciousness. Ego Conscious-ness is the avenue along which all must travel who want wisdom, wealth and power.

Egoism is the greatest good to the greatest man, or the wis-est organism. It is Nature's way. She rewards the one who strug-gles and strives towards Self Consciousness; and punishes the lazy, the apathetic and contented Ego.

• • •

Every person has two distinct minds—objective and subjec-tive. Our objective mind acts consciously on sensations and ideas which come to us from the outside world. It is under the governing power of our will. Our subjective mind acts uncon-sciously on the instinctive impressions which spring from our inner consciousness.

Ego Conscious Egoist seeks to become better acquainted with these two states of consciousness, and thus increase the power of his Ego.

• • •

Is man a social animal? No! Because if he were, there would be no lynching. No jails or penitentiaries.

Man is not a political animal, or men and women would

have had the ballot as soon as government began.

Man is not a religious animal, or there would never have been massacres, inquisitions, martyrs, religious wars, crusades, Peter-the-Hermits, and Mohammet, who enforced his religion by the sword.

Man is not a moral animal or there would be no humbugs, swindlers or murderers. Man becomes moral through sheer self-interest and because it pays.

Education along egoistic lines will make mankind moral, social, and really sane.

• • •

Altruism, Christianity, Socialism, Communism, Bolshevism, Brotherhood of Man, with Equality, Fraternity, Liberty, are all impossible until man has learned how to socialize his selfishness, which means that he finds pleasure in giving away the surplus value of his ego.

The Great Affirmative

Jesus, the great Egoist, said: "I am the Way, the Truth, and the Light; only through me can you attain eternal life,"[010] and yet there are millions of Christians who have not found themselves out—from within.

Civilization is ages old, but it has found no certain way of putting wisdom on her thrones and eternal truth in her seats of power.

Could anything be more strange, after 10,000 years of human history, after centuries of literature and learning and progress, than that millions do not yet understand the fundamental laws of Nature?

Self-interest rules the world, and selfishness the individual.

The cause of all the trouble in the world is because selfishness is running riot in the hearts and thoughts of men and women. Selfishness righteously handled can be made the source of all good.

---

010   John 14:6

The socialization of selfishness is the remedy for the ills of the ego, and of the world.

• • •

Something is holding humanity down to the animal plane of existence; what is it? Ignorant selfishness. Something in all the times has prevented spiritual psychic progress from keeping pace with material progress; what is it? Ignorant selfishness or lack of psychic wisdom.

If it is clearly demonstrable that man can be taught to do selfish acts that will bring happiness to others, and while so doing, be happy doing it, then we may say that selfishness is a social factor in producing harmony and concord among mankind. In fact, it his the only way that systematic and permanent concord can be found and found only among Ego Conscious or self-conscious organisms.

• • •

As machinery will soon be cheaper than poor humanity, the working class as a class will be abolished. Civilization will then be possible, because man will have time to think, and logical thought will make him an Ego Conscious organism. Enlightened selfishness will do the rest, whatever it may be. Salvation by selfishness is the only Natural solution for all problems.

Egoism is the Baptism of the brain in the water of wisdom.

• • •

Education only can regulate selfishness and eradicate ignorance.

• • •

Sympathy is the sublime part of selfishness, for Sympathy for others is pity for self. Sympathy is therefore self-pity. Self-pity is self-love in a state of righteous fermentation. Self-pity is the law that makes sympathy possible; Sympathy is the law that expresses itself in Congeniality. Congeniality is the law that produces Fellowship, and Fellowship is the law of Concord and Affinity, and Affinity is the law of Attraction and Attachment.

●●●

Selfishness preserves and perpetuates the Ego. Hate protects and regulates the Ego; Vanity makes for the power and progress of the Ego, for the time being. Selfishness is the dynamo of destiny; hate the dynamo of destruction and death, when recklessly handled; Vanity is the dynamo of success; and love the dynamo of desire. These four forces of good or evil, may be productive of good when manipulated by the Ego Conscious Supercrat. Their baneful influence is seen only when they control the actions of ignorant organisms.

Quotations

"We are Naturally regardless of the effect of our conduct on others. We have no innate love for our fellows. The highest virtue is not without regard, it has a satisfaction of its own, the pleasure of contemplating one's own worth."[011]

—Mandeville.

"One must be vain or conceited about something; otherwise life becomes a bore and a burden—sometimes a tragedy."

"Every one of us is born with a genius for Egotism to keep us from discovering how futile and foolish we are."

—Corra Harris.

"None loves another as itself nor venerates another so, nor is it possible, thought a greater than itself, to know."

—W. Blake.

Mandeville says: "Pride and vanity have built more hospitals than all the virtues together. It is the chief ingredient in the chastity of women and in the courage of men."

"Wisdom is to speak the truth and consciously to act according to Nature."[012]

—Heraclitus.

"How shall we learn to know ourselves? By reflection? Never: but only thru action: Strive to do thy duty; then shalt thou know what is in thee."

—Goethe.

"There is a space between every atom. Self is always selfish."[013]

—Lord Lytton.

---

011 Bernard de Mandeville (1670 - 1733). Author. Quote from "An Essay on Charity, and Charity-Schools."
012 Heraclitus (c535 - c475 BC). Philosopher.
013 Lord Edward George Earle Lytton Bulwer-Lytton, 1st Baron Lytton (1803 - 1873). Quote from *Kenelm Chillingly.*

The Ego

The Ego. *(from the Greek meaning* I.*)*

"I am not an Ego along with other Egoes, but the Sole
Ego; I am unique!"[014]

—Max Stirner.

Every Conscious Ego can say:
(1) I am, I am myself, I am I.
(2) I am conscious of present state with ability to
differentiate, and separate the past from the present,
and with power to mould the future to some extent.
(3) I am conscious of continuity of existence. I am
capable of testing the pulse of personality and of
registering the added consciousness of the Ego.

These are the three infallible states of being.
The Conscious Egoist can also say:
I believe in myself. I know that I am. I know I am I.
You and me. There's a difference. I am me. I am I. Some
philosophers are full of perplexing and tormenting
subtleties to prove that no man really knows whether
he is or isn't; that all outward things exist merely as
mental images, and that you and I are only fragments
of our imaginations. This idea may be relegated to
the waste-paper basket, because no matter what
philosophers may say, I know that I am myself.

I know when I have the toothache I feel the pain
and nobody else can gauge accurately the degree of
agony I endure. In this respect I am apart from all
things. I suffer while other people look on. I know the

---

014   *The Ego and Its Own.*

difference between pleasure and pain. I know what I like and what I dislike. I know what I want and don't want. I can think and I can plan a program covering a day, a month, a year. I can see into the future.

I can stand erect and look back and forward, capitalizing experience, predicting the future on my memory of the past, using the illuminating power of imagination to prepare the program of the future and preceding by my own will to make my dreams come true. So can everybody else!

• • •

The Ego is a world in himself; the center of sensations: a microcosm in a macrocosm.

An Ego is the *rendezvous* of reason, revelations, realties, and self-realizations.

The Ego has the faculty of seeing additions to itself, the ability to analyze these additions and thus to increase Ego Consciousness by becoming more aware of his former and newly acquired consciousness.

He becomes a Self-conscious, Ego Conscious organism with a tendency to preserve himself, to realize himself. He is aware of himself. His chief concern is himself. The more self-conscious, or Ego Conscious, he becomes, the more he becomes capable of taking care of himself.

Egoism is the law of the Ego. It is a secret of man, not a secret of Nature; because Nature exposes her purpose in the actions of every human being, and every other living thing.

The Voice of Nature fails all those who can hear that the purpose of life is to satisfy one's strongest craving—for the moment—on the part of the unconscious Egoist; and to gratify one's greatest ambition on the part of the Ego Conscious Supercrat—like a Lindbergh[015] or a Napoleon.

---

015   Charles Augustus Lindbergh (1902 - 1974). Aviator. Flew solo from New York to Paris in the year *Gospel...* was published.

This is the reason why the Subterman travels along the line of least resistance, and finds failure and sometimes slavery, while the Supercrat travels along the line of most resistance and greatest attraction, and finds new sensations, and the thrills of new dangers, which bring wisdom and inspirations. Supercratic Egoism or Enlightened Self-Interest will solve all the problems that are perplexing mankind today. Taking Nature's laws as a guide the enlightened Egoist will do the right thing in the right way at the right time—out of sheer selfishness—thus producing the greatest possible good with the least expenditure of labor, either mental or physical.

When necessary to their interests, Egoists will cooperate, because it will add to their prosperity and power.

• • •

Everybody is an Ego and an Egoist, sometimes an Egotist. There are two kinds of Egos, the conscious, and the unconscious. The conscious Egoist is a Supercrat. The unconscious Egoist is a mass of matter that doesn't matter much, except when exploited.

Two Kinds of Egos

The Egoist is Vain, Ego Conscious, Wise with surplus value.

The Egotist is Conceited, Unconscious, Foolish, with surplus energy of little value.

• • •

Unconscious Egos are enemies to themselves because their emotions are stronger than their reason. They are hewers of wood and drawers of water, because they have no psychic insight, being aware only of their deficiencies, and inability to express themselves, lack self-control when their emotions are aroused or outraged. On the other hand, the Ego Conscious Egoist, or Egocrat, knows his own limitations. He is aware that all motives have their root in Selfishness, and believes that selfishness is eternal, hate infernal, love internal, and vanity is external in expression and in deed. He predicates that Love is the most selfish of the emotions, hate the most tragic, and vanity the most dramatic.

He can audit his own agonies; minimize misery, macerate malice, annihilate anger, manufacture mirth, pulverize his own prejudices and paralyze his own paralogies, because he has found himself out from within.

Knowing all these things he affirms that only enlightened Selfishness can rescue mankind—or part of it—from ignorance, poverty, crime, disease, and early death.

• • •

There are two other kinds of Egoists: the unscrupulous, or anti-social, and the scrupulous, or social Egoist.

The Social Supercrat possesses these qualities: Psychic Sagacity, Dynamic Capacity, Social Instinct, Intuition of Intellect, Will to Wisdom, Will to Power, and is Scrupulous.

The Exploitative Supercrat possesses these qualities: Psychic Sagacity, Dynamic Capacity, Mental Audacity, Perspicacious Pugnacity, Intuition of Intellect, Will to Power, and is Unscrupulous.

The unscrupulous Egoist is a great exploiter, but is progressive in tendency; the social Egoist is also a great exploiter, but is civilizing in his effect. Both work from the same motive—for self-gratification—but with different results. Both recognize that exploitation is the first law of individual and industrial progress, and profit thereby.

These are the pioneers of wealth production, and the pace-makers of prosperity, progress and power.

• • •

There are two kinds of public benefactors: the Fordanthropist[016] and the Philanthropist. The Fordanthropist gives away his joys in the form of high wages and short hours to his workers, and the Philanthropist, who gives away his griefs in the form of hospitals, churches and free libraries. The first is a scientist with a

---

016   Henry Ford (1863 - 1947). Industrialist.

vision, the second is a sciolist with a decision.

Fordanthropist socializes his joys; the Philanthropist collectivizes his agonies. The enlightened selfishness of the former creates new conditions and brings prosperity to millions of men and women, while the crude selfishness of the latter tends to perpetuate conditions and produce apathy and patience on the part of the poor.

• • •

Happiness and misery are made out of the same materials.

All evil is wrought by want of thought by ignorant and anti-social Egos; all good is brought about by the action of wise Egos who have socialized their selfishness and given away the surplus value of their Ego with judgment and joy. The mean creature expresses his selfishness in a mean manner. The noble Ego displays his Ego in a noble manner. Both act from the same motive, self-gratification, which is selfishness.

• • •

Man never does anything except for self-approval or self-gratification. He is interested in everything he does. There is no such thing as disinterested action. He never does anything that will bring remorse. Remorse comes afterwards, because the result of the action is unsatisfactory to the doer. Remorse is the aftermath of folly. Folly is the foolish gratification of emotion or desire for the moment. A man gives a beggar a dime for the pleasure or kick he gets out of it. When a man passes a beggar and then turns back to give him something, he does so to ease his mind and feelings. He expresses his sympathy in this way, because he is full of self-pity at the sight of the beggar; for sympathy for others is pity for self. By giving he finds relief and passes along at peace with himself.

All human beings are Egoists and individualists and selfish. They can't be otherwise, because the aim of life is personal gratification. All desire to gratify their Egoistic yearnings. It is necessary for such things to be, otherwise the race would die out and humanity would become extinct. The desire to be happy in one's own way is inborn. It can't be destroyed.

Each seeks his own happiness and conflict arises from the opposition of men's desires.

Hume says: "As some men have not the turn of imagination, and others have, this alone is quite enough to make the widest difference of human character, and to stamp one man as virtuous and humane, and another vicious and merely interested."

• • •

If most individuals or Egos were consciously and Supercratically selfish, deception would be decreased to a minimum; sanity would be increased to the maximum, and poverty, misery, crime and suffering would be diminished to decimal fractions.

• • •

It is not the good but the evil qualities of men that lead to worldly greatness. Without luxury we should have no trade, for vanity is the foundation of all finery and luxurious leanings.

• • •

The prevailing and popular doctrine is that the human mind possesses an intuition or instinct, whereby we feel or discern at once the right from the wrong, a view termed the doctrine of the moral sense, or Moral Sentiment. Mandeville claims that self-interest is the only test of moral righteousness.

The utilitarians suppose that the well-being or happiness of mankind is the sole end and ultimate standard of morality, the greatest good to the greatest number.

Enlightened Egoism will abolish sin, for sin is simply ignorance running riot in the realm of raw realities. Where reason reigns supreme, sanity will be as common as ignorance is today.

There will be no remorse in the mind of an Enlightened Ego for any action done in the past. Mistakes may be made, but remorse will not he the aftermath for there will arise a determination to do better in the future.

• • •

Civilization consists of Egos grouping according to temperament, and on the same plane of consciousness. In this way concord can be attained and success sustained. The atoms of attraction must be free to find each other before they can congregate according to congeniality and a true measure of friendship and fellowship can be found.

• • •

The Egoism of the ignorant Egoist is expressed through intolerance, bigotry and cruelty.

The bigot says: "Believe as I do, or be damned," etc.

The Egoism of the Conscious Egoist is tinctured with tolerance, consideration, and a sense of proportion, because the outcome of a sane argument or action may be of more value in the future than to insist on preserving present values.

If the Egoist is weak his egoism is worthless. If the Egoist is strong, acute, full of distinctive character, his egoism is precious, and remains a possession of the race.

The Unconscious Egoist is oblivious to the obvious therefore powerless—except to destroy.

As Nietzsche says: "Selfishness has as much value as the psychological value of him who possesses it; it may be very valuable, or it may be very vile and contemptible."[017]

The fool would expose himself in all his meanness, thereby giving himself away, so that others would be aware of his presence and be able to avoid him in the future—unless he improved in conduct. The wise man should multiply, because enlightened Egoism would make it fashionable to be oneself.

To be oneself demands self-knowledge and self-control.

The religion of service would be popular among conscious Egoists. Self-interest would demand it. High class service by High class Egoists.

Emulation, without envy, would reign righteously, bringing

---

017   Friedrich Nietzsche (1844 - 1900). Philosopher. Quote from *The Will to Power*.

about the survival of the fittest—to live, to laugh, to love, and to rule.

• • •

The Explorative Supercrat is the creator of new values and new systems.

He moulds the multitude with his own matrix, for his will is the guiding star to their own slavery.

The Social Supercrat is the creator of a new Social consciousness, and a new civilization, for he dispenses his surplus value with prodigal power as a conscious evolutionary Egoist.

It pays to be kind and considerate to your friends and neighbors.

It pays to be courteous and conscientious in your intercourse with others.

It pays to be honest and straightforward in your dealings with others.

It pays to cultivate a true sense of proportion, so that you can be just to others as you are to yourself.

It pays to be a Supercrat in thought, an Aristocrat in action and a Superman in embryo—both morally, socially, and psychologically.

Quotations

"The wise have no doubts; the virtuous, no sorrows; the brave, no fears."

—Confucius.

"Hear ye these words! For, though they may appear as measured rhyming to the heedless ear, they try to voice the teachings of a Seer who, seeing, knew."

—*A Sage's Soliloquy*.

"Man centers everything in himself, and neither loves nor hates, but for his own sake."

—Mandeville.

"I have unbounded faith in what is called human selfishness. I know no other foundation to build upon. When we cease quarreling with this indestructible instinct of self-preservation and learn to use it as one of the greatest forces of Nature, it will be found to work beneficently for all mankind, and the stone which has been rejected by the builders will become the chief cornerstone."

—Mrs. E. D. Linton.[018]

"Egoism is everywhere, for everything is Egoism."

"To me there is no such thing as Altruism—that is, the doing of anything wholly for the good of others. We do things for self-satisfaction."

—J. A. Labadie.[019]

---

018   E. D. Linton. Quote from *The Eagle and the Serpent* No. 18, in turn quoting *Liberty*.
019   Charles Joseph Antoine "Jo" Labadie (1850 - 1933). Anarchist and archivist. Quote from *The Eagle and the Serpent* No. 18, in turn quoting his periodical *Liberty*.

"God and mankind have concerned themselves for nothing, for nothing but themselves. Let me then, likewise, concern myself for myself, who am equally with God the nothing of all others, who am my all, who am the only one."

—M. Stirner.

"Prejudice, vanity, calculation, these are what govern the world."

—Chamfort.[020]

"The self-conscious Ego is the essential basis of social re-generation."

—Tak Kak.

"Every person possesses in himself his greatest enemy, and at the same time his greatest friend—his own Ego."

—Dr. Stekel.[021]

"The world's greatest Super-Egoists; they are responsible for all progress since man developed a thumb."

"Two men look out through the bars / One sees the mud, and one sees the stars."

—F. Landbridge.[022]

020   Sébastien-Roch Nicolas, aka Chamfort (1741 - 1794). Author.
021   Wilhelm Stekel (1868 - 1940). Psychologist. Quote from *The Beloved Ego* (1921).
022   Frederick Langbridge (1849 – 1922). Author. Popularized but did not originate quote.

Egoism: Conscious and Unconscious

"My diet masculine is having its effect—my sayings of power and vigor. I feed men, not with flatulent vegetables but with warrior food."

—Nietzsche.[023]

1

"The maintenance of civilisation depends on nearly all people being fools."

—H. N. Dickenson.[024]

"Man is as heaven made him, and something a great deal worse."

—Cervantes.[025]

"The public is not a philosopher."

—Jules Lemaitre.

"The bad men of the world are occupied in undoing the evil wrought by the good."

• • •

Certain men, who have had the courage to probe down to the very bottom of their own minds, have come to the conclusion that self-interest is the one motive of all human action; I might say of all action that is not merely mechanical and has life at the root of it.

This belief, conviction, or conclusion—term it what you will—forms the whole sum and substance of the philosophy called "Egoism," and the man who, after due reflection, subscribes himself to it, becomes a "Conscious Egoist;" conscious! mark you—in that alone lies the difference between himself

---

023   Quote from *Thus Spake Zarathustra*.
024   Humphrey Neville Dickinson (c1882 - 1916). Author. Quote from *Things that Are Caesar's*.
025   Miguel de Cervantes Saavedra (1547 – 1616). Author. Quote from *Don Quixote de la Mancha* Book 4.

and the unbeliever; or, according to his philosophy, all men are Egoists by an inevitable law—the Supreme Law of Nature!

The question is then, with regard to Egoism, not "Are you an Egoist?" but "Are you conscious of the fact that you are an Egoist?" Call yourself what you will, if you are not a Conscious Egoist, you are merely an unconscious one.

This may seem a revoltingly dogmatic philosophy to those who are still floundering about in the shallows of ancient reasoning, like little boys just learning to swim and afraid to go more than a yard or so beyond the land. But let these good people come out into the broad sea of self, let them realise their own Nature, find what is best and most pleasing within them, draw it out to the full, and not be ashamed to say, or think, that by so doing they are serving self and self merely; then, in the opinion of the Conscious Egoist, they will become wise and sensible beings.

The Conscious Egoist asserts that all actions of all men are taken either in the quest of happiness or in the avoidance of pain. This is the groundwork upon which he builds up his reasoning.

Says he:

> Whenever a man performs what the world might term a self sacrifice, either he finds pleasure in it or avoids pain. For instance, the philanthropist who spends his time and money in relieving the poor and needy, does it either to gain the pleasure or self-satisfaction of having done a good and charitable action, or to avoid the pain, as far as it is possible, of seeing his fellow-creatures suffer.[026]

Or take another instance, that of the man who risks or definitely sacrifices his own life to save that of some other person. Either he does it from a Natural desire to be courageous, or else the thought of seeing another creature die is more painful to

---

026   Morse Monroe. Quote from "Egoism: Conscious and Unconscious" in *The Eagle and The Serpent* Volume 2 Number 5, September 1902.

him than is the thought of dying himself.

Hence we see that in two instances the term "self-sacrifice" is not admissible; for both the Philanthropist and the Hero are plainly serving and not sacrificing self.

The Altruist (who is merely an unconscious Egoist) will most strenuously deny this because it would hurt his vanity to admit that his own actions are self-serving and not self-sacrificing. Says he, "It is possible to do an action which shall give pleasure to or detract from the pain of another, and yet neither attain pleasure oneself or avoid pain in the doing of it. Rather the reverse," he argues. "It will detract from one's own pleasure, and add to the burden of one's own pain."

"And yet," says the Conscious Egoist, "You would assert that Virtue is its own reward?"

"Yes, I would," says the Altruist.

"And you are more pleased, let us say satisfied, in being what you call unselfish than you would be if you knew you were what is called selfish?" the Conscious Egoist questions.

"Certainly," says the Altruist.

"Then," says the Conscious Egoist with a smile, "Your Altruism (which you call unselfishness) is merely the outcome of selfishness. Do you see the contradiction?"

The Altruist shakes his head. He will not part with his false philosophy so easily. He has grown to love it because it has flattered his individuality by representing his action to be that which they are not. "I fail to see your point," he says in an emphatic voice, as though his failing to see a thing proved that the thing was not there to be seen. And the Conscious Egoist is seized with an exceeding great pity for the Altruist, who is very blind indeed.

2

You will observe that I am sticking to the phrase "Conscious

Egoist" in alluding to the believer in Egoism. The whole virtue of reasoning upon the subject lies in that word "conscious," which so many professed Egoists forget to prefix to themselves when arguing with the benighted ones. Says the Conscious Egoist very often to the so-called Altruist, "I am an Egoist and you are an Egoist; there is no difference between us." And the Altruist at once thinks that there is something wrong with the statement, for he sees a great difference somewhere, though he hardly knows where it is. And in this instance the Altruist is right. Both men are Egoists, certainly, and yet there is a difference between them. The one is a Conscious Egoist, the other a very unconscious one. In the case of one Egoism is recognized, in the case of the other it is strongly denied, although it exists just the same.

Here the Altruist might throw in what would seem to him a weighty argument. "There is," he might say, "a greater difference between man and man than this consciousness and unconsciousness. For instance, between two persons who call themselves Conscious Egoists there may be a vast difference. The one may be a fairly good fellow, one to be tolerated in spite of his opinions, while another may be a rogue, a vagabond, and a disagreeable fellow to boot. How do you account for that?" Very easily. The difference in this case is the difference that is always between man and man, and it lies in a man's ego or self, and not in his Egoism, which is merely the Natural law of the ego. The ego of a man, or his individuality, is more or less limited. He is born strong in certain powers and weak in others. Even his mentality is never perfect. Sometimes a portion of it will attain or closely approach perfection, and then the man is called a genius; but this development of one portion is nearly always at the expense of another portion. Hence is genius so irregular. Well, there being, as I have said, a difference between man and man, and all men being, by a law of Nature. Egoists, it stands to reason that the difference between man and man is the difference between Egoist and Egoist. The same difference would be apparent if all men had the misfortune to be born Altruists (which is an impossible supposition as in reality Altruism is only an imaginative quality). But supposing that Dame Nature for a moment changed the unchangeable law, and in a fit of cruelty made all men Altruists; I doubt whether she would have the consistency to make them all alike.

Thus, the only thing in which men may not differ, according to the philosophy of Egoism, is motive. This alone is unchangeable. Christ dying in agony on the Cross, and the drunken wife-beater beating his wife to death in a fit of passion, are inspired by one and the same motive—self-satisfaction. Christ felt that out of respect for Himself, or for His principles, which means the same thing, He most suffer this terrible death. The wife-beater feels that out of respect for himself he must assert his mastery over his wife.

That is the way I look at it.

"But," argues the Altruist, "if you assert that their motives are the same, you seem to me to be putting Christ and the wife-beater on a level. I fail to see how you can make any distinction between them."

Answers the Conscious Egoist, "As I have said before, the difference lies in the men themselves, and not in their motives. One man may delight in pleasing others, while the other delights in displeasing others. In this case they will act oppositely, though from a similar motive. It is right and logical to call a man a good man or a bad man; but it is wrong and illogical to assert that there are good motives and bad motives."

A man is a good man or a bad man in our eyes accordingly as we are pleased or displeased by his behavior. Thus all difference is relative, and we judge an object by the relation that object bears to ourselves. This is why the world loves its Saviours, its

Messiahs, its Prophets, its Martyrs, its geniuses, its great inventors and discoverers—simply because they have benefited the world. Gratitude is very clearly the outcome of selfishness, like all the virtues.

3

I am not here to defend that which the world calls selfishness, and condemns so strongly, in theory that is. I also would condemn it; yet I would not call it selfishness, but narrowness, littleness, baseness. The man who is commonly called selfish is no more selfish then the rest of his brethren; but his mind is stunted, his conception of himself is too limited. His joys are petty, his sorrows are mean. He has misconceived himself.

The secret of good and bad egoism lies in the ego's conception of itself. A man may be conscious of his egoism, and yet sublimely unconscious of a great part of his ego or self. The body has its needs and the mind has its needs. These needs are many and various, and a man must grasp them all, and strive to satisfy them ere he becomes a perfect Egoist. This seems almost an impossible task—a task for God, not for man of flesh and blood and imperfections. But we can try.

It is an unconscious recognition of his own mental need which turns a man to what he calls Altruism. It is a recognition (conscious or unconscious) of mental need which makes a man love honesty, justice, mercy and charity. It is a recognition, again, of mental need, which gives man a longing for wholeness and Continence of body and mind, and breeds in him the thing called morality. Also it is a his own mental need which makes a man rebel against the lack of proportion that exist today in society. He sees one person suffering from want of that which is absolutely necessary to him if he is to live, while another has all that he can wish for, both of the necessities and the superfluities of life. He feels that there is something wrong with the world;

and feels also, perhaps without realising that he does it, that the world is part of himself just as much as he is part of the world. Therefore he strives to right the world, because only when the world is perfect can he himself be perfect. Is this unselfishness? Clearly not. It is a broad, enlightened selfishness, which has widened out self so that it includes the whole universe of things. A magnificent selfishness, but not altruism.

<h1 style="text-align:center">4</h1>

Usually the Altruist takes Jesus of Nazareth as his pattern to live or to perish by; and he argues that Christ preached and practiced the doctrine of complete self-abnegation.

This is a conclusion which can only he arrived at by those who have halted half-way in their reasoning. Christ did not preach the doctrine of complete self-abnegation. He may have imagined and even declared Himself to have been doing so; but in that case He could not have fully grasped the import of His own doctrine. What Christ really advocated was the abnegation (complete if you like) of one half of self to the other half, of the physical self to the purely mental, or if you will (for to me the two words have a synonymous meaning) spiritual self.

Christ considered that half of man was good and half was evil, and that these two halves of man made perpetual war upon each other. One of them, said He, must conquer in the end and trample the other underfoot, the which depending upon the will of the individual. He preached that it was best for the individual that his evil self should He stifled and his good self cultivated to its fullest extent. Rather a one sided doctrine to him who recognises that only that what is evil to an individual which is positively hurtful; yet let us examine it to find whether there is in it a trace of genuine unselfishness.

We find that men are advised to be unselfish because it is best for themselves that they be so, to crush self because self will benefit by it. Clearly, if a man does what is best for himself for the reason that it is best for himself, he is mistaken in calling his action unselfish.

Therefore the term Altruist is a misnomer, even when applied to practical Christianity.

5

As I have said before, these are two kinds of selfishness, the broad and the narrow. Let me illustrate this by giving you two types of men, first the man who is narrowly selfish, then the man whose selfishness is broad and enlightened.

We will suppose both men to be earnestly religious; the supposition is not an improbable one.

The first man, on the promises of the Bible, sacrifices himself, as he believes, on Earth, for the sake of an eternity of aesthetic bliss in Heaven. He can never lose sight of the promised reward—if he did he would cease to be religious. His every act of charity is done because he knows that it will be returned to him a thousandfold. I make hold to say that this man is the most common type of religionist. He has taken the narrow view of religion, regarding it as an unpleasant means towards ultimate pleasure.

The broadly religious man believes in and follows a religion for its own sake, at the bottom reckless of eternity. "This religion," he says, "will benefit me here, on earth. It will bring me nearer to what I would wish to here. I am most happy when I am doing good, because I know that it is good. If doing good will take me to Heaven, very well. If not, it has gone towards making a Heaven on Earth."

The Conscious Egoist, regarding these two believers would assert that both were inspired by the same motive, the attainment of self-satisfaction, but there, most probably, the similarity ends, for each goes a different way about it according to his lights. The one whose mind is narrow and ill-lighted may attain a mean kind of pleasure at a great loss. The one whose mind is broad, open and enlightened may gain infinite pleasure at less cost to himself.

6

I hold that if a man makes a sacrifice he does not, nay, cannot. sacrifice himself wholly; but merely sacrifice one part of himself to another part.

It is a law of evolution that the fittest mental attributes as well as the fittest physical attributes should survive; and it is this survival of the fittest which we call the victory of right over wrong, or reason over prejudice.

Man is a creature of conflicting passions; and it is best or fittest, for the world that those passions, or impulses, should survive in the struggle which are most congenial or beneficial to the world as a whole; and it is for the individual that he should be in compete harmony with the world and the world's spirit, otherwise, like an obstinate cog-wheel in a rapidly whirling machine, he is apt to get broken and to fly off at a tangent, a useless article. Or else, if he is particularly strong as well as particularly obstinate, the machine, by which I signify the world's progress, may be stayed for a while until a stronger power than himself removes him and his influence.

7

But I have wandered a little from the direct course of my reasoning.

You see, though Egoism is such a vast subject, it does not stand much description. The shorter the description of Egoism, the better and clearer it will be. One might sum it up neatly in a little aphorism, "Egoism is everything, for everything is Egoism." This is what the Conscious Egoist advances against the idea of Altruism. He says, "I could prove to you, if there was time enough in the course of a lifetime to do so, that everything in the world and out of it is Egoism or the result of Egoism. I have proved it to myself already, and such being the case, I do not see how Altruism can exist. There is no room for it. In a vessel that is quite full of one substance there is no room for another."

8

The thing which causes most misunderstanding between the Conscious Egoist and the Unconscious Egoist is that the Unconscious Egoist looks upon Egoism as a doctrine preached by the Conscious Egoist, whereas it is an inevitable fact merely stated by him.

The difference between a fact and doctrine should be plain to everyone. And yet I have heard it said by people who might reasonably claim to be intelligent that there is no real difference between them. But if a fact and a doctrine are merely one and the same thing, how do you account for the multitudinous number of facts that were in existence ere ever a doctrine was preached or invented? A doctrine is a structure of reasoning raised upon a foundation of fact. The reasoning may be correct or fallacious, but this has nothing to do with the fact upon which it is based. If the doctrine is wrong, and mankind becomes conscious that it is wrong, then the doctrine will die out: but the fact remains, and another doctrine, more in harmony with it, will be raised upon its foundation.

Were Egoism a doctrine, the Conscious Egoist would approach you with these words. "Be selfish, for it is best that you should be so." Instead of which, he comes to you and says, "You are selfish, you cannot help it. Therefore you had better recognize the fact."

I say again, Egoism is given forth as a fact and not as a doctrine. The Conscious Egoist asks a man to look into himself and recognize that which is within him. "Man, know thyself." If I do a good action it is the result of Egoism. If I do a bad action, it is the result of Egoism. I am brave by reason—of my Egoism, and cowardly by the same reason.

9

Egoism, then, is merely a mental force which makes a man move, and keeps him moving. It rests with a man's ego in which direction he will move. Men have good egos and bad egos; strong, healthy egos, and weak, morbid, unhealthy egos. Egoism is not the ego but the law of the ego.

Difference in men's actions is no sign of difference in their motives. It is simply a proof of difference, either inborn or cultivated, in the men themselves. Therefore there is no unreasonableness in saying that good actions and bad actions (by which I mean actions beneficial to the world and actions detrimental to it) are inspired by Egoism, the mere realisation of self.

10

A question was asked in my hearing some little time ago of a lecturer in sympathy with the philosophy of Egoism, which hardly received an adequate answer, the fault being that the answer was too concise and unexplanatory to be convincing to the mind of the inquirer. The lecturer forgot that the inquirer looked at matters in quite a different light to himself, or else he realized that he had not sufficient time to begin at the root of the matter and lead upward.

The question was, as far as I remember, "If Universal Egoism is a fact, how do you account for that feeling of benevolence towards others which exists in the human mind?"

I forget the lecturer's exact reply, but I know that the inquirer was eminently unsatisfied; and I will try myself to answer the question as fully as I can, and as clearly; and, if the inquirer should read these words, I sincerely hope I shall satisfy him that, taking Egoism fully into consideration, the feeling of benevolence he alludes to is not entirely unaccountable.

In the first place, what is this feeling of benevolence? Looked at logically, it is simply a desire for the expansion of self. When there is another person. seemingly outside yourself, whose joys and sorrows affect you just as much as do your own, it is equivalent to your having two selves, for this person's very life becomes a part of your life. Therefore to strive to make that other person happy is to strive to make yourself happy at the same time, because, by reason of your extension of self, you cannot he perfectly happy unless he is in similar condition.

This is what benevolence practically amounts to, whether it is on a large scale, and (as it does in some highly developed egos) embraces the whole human race, or whether it is on a small scale, and embraces a narrow circle of acquaintances.

Take, for instance, that man whose love is so strong that he will lay down his life to save one he loves. It is because of his love that he does it, and what is this love? It is the merging of his own life completely into the life of another, so completely, that at the time of his apparent self-sacrifice the body which he gave to destruction, his own body, he felt instinctively to contain less of himself than that which he was desirous of saving.

Benevolence is a mild form of love, mild because it is widely diffused. A man with a great capacity for loving may, accordingly as he is circumstanced, concentrate his love upon a single individual, or scatter it abroad among the sons of men. Or he may shed it equally over all living things, as Buddha is said to have done, who voluntarily gave his own body to be a feast for a starving tigress and her cubs, because he could not bear to see their sufferings—the greatest sacrifice I have heard of, even in mythology.

You will admit that one does pleasure in acts of benevolence, that one is always glad to see those one loves happy and contented. I do not see how you can deny it. And when one is happy, or pleased, it is because one's ego—or self—is to a certain extent satisfied. Therefore self-satisfaction is quite consistent with benevolence and self-satisfaction is another word for Egoism.

To conclude, let me restate my case as briefly as possible. I have said:

(1) That all actions of all men are taken in order to satisfy the cravings of the ego, or self. Therefore all men are Egoists.

(2) That some are conscious of the fact and some are unconscious of the fact.

(3) That among the unconscious ones there are those who assert that it is possible to be the opposite of Egoist, to wit Altruist, and that it is a man's duty to the Altruist rather than Egoist.

(4) That this is an impossible theory, because the very thing which they call Altruism springs out of and is nothing more or less than a form of Egoism.

(5) That there is no such thing as self-sacrifice; that the man who gives his life to save another values his life less than that other, or he would not do it.

(6) That to say all men are Egoists does not put them on a level. It merely gives them a common motive. Widely different actions may spring from this motive. The difference, where there is one, lies in a man's ego, or self.

Egoism is the law of the ego.

The Gospel According to Malfew Seklew

(7) That Egoism is a fact which cannot be escaped from, not a doctrine which may be followed out at will; and it is best and most honest to recognize this fact, thereby becoming a Conscious Egoist. The motto for the Conscious Egoist is "Man, Know Thyself, or "Find Thyself Out."

(8) That all those actions which it behooves a man to do who would call himself an Altruist may be done by a man who would call himself a Conscious Egoist, without the slightest inconsistency. The only difference between the two men in that case would be that the Conscious Egoist was more alive to the Nature of himself than was the Altruist.

Quotations

"A few are fighting for Truths that are too newly-born to the world of Consciousness to have any considerable number of people on their side as yet."[027]

—Ibsen.

"The Ego defends and demands its own."

—C. K. Chesterton.

"Bad examples may be as profitable to virtue as good ones."

—Montagne.

"All the pleasures die with the years except self-love."

—Voltaire.

"Self-love is a strange counsellor; it generally disagrees with reason and as often carries the day."[028]

—George Sand.

"Wisdom is the principal thing; therefore get wisdom."[029]

—The Bible.

"We are making progress in things; are we making progress in men?"

"It will, by and by, be found out that a knowledge of the laws of life is more important than any other knowledge."

—H. Spencer.

---

027   Henrik Ibsen (1828 - 1906), Playwright. Quote from *An Enemy of the People*.
028   Amantine-Lucile-Aurore Dupin (1804 - 1876). Author. Quote from *Lady Blake's Love Letters*.
029   Proverbs 4:7

"Knowledge comes, but wisdom lingers."[030]

          —Tennyson.

There's but the twinkling of a star
Between a man of peace and war;
A thief and justice, fool and knave,
A huffing officer and a slave,
A crafty lawyer and a pickpocket,
A great philosopher and a blockhead,
A formal preacher and a player,
A learned physician and a man-slayer.

          —Butler.

"All that has gone to make the greatness of civilizations, sciences, arts, philosophies, religions, military power, etc., has been the working of individuals with great minds—Supercrats."[031]

          —LeBon.

"The greatest virtues are only splendid sins."

          —St. Augustine.

"To increase the care in creatures to preserve themselves, Nature has given them an instinct by which every individual values itself above its real value."

          —Mandeville.

---

030   Alfred Tennyson, 1st Baron Tennyson (1809 - 1892). Poet. Coined the phrase "Nature, red in tooth and claw." Quote from *Locksley Hall*.

031   Gustave LeBon (1841-1931). Quote from *Psychologie du Socialisme*. Seklew alters the quote and inserts his own "Supercrats" terminology here. The original quote, translated, should read "...work of individuals and not collectives."

The original does go on to say "It is by favoured individuals, the rare and supreme fruits of a few superior races, that the most important discoveries and advances, by which all humanity profits, have been realised. The peoples among whom Individualism is most highly developed are by this fact alone at the head of civilisation, and today dominate the world," certainly this is encapsulted in his term "Supercrats".

Planes of Ego Consciousness
(From the Epistle to a Creative Evolutionist)

The Plane of Human Consciousness is that plane of conscious activity which is manifested by human beings, high and low, in varying degrees. The very lowest forms of human consciousness, and man's mental and emotional activity, is but little more than that of the higher animals—in fact, in some cases the animals actually seem to display a greater degree of intellectual power, though on instinctive lines. But even in the lowest forms of human life there appears at least a faint glimmering of Self Consciousness, or the conviction that "I am I," that form of consciousness by means of which the human individual becomes aware of himself as an individual entity. This, rather than the degree of intellectual development, is the characteristic distinguishing mark of the human being.

In the case of the highest animals the consciousness is always directed outward, but in even the lowest type of man there is at least a faint degree of the inward of consciousness. The animal always thinks of outside things, while even the primitive man occasionally thinks of himself—makes himself the object of his own thought in at least the sense of considering his own feelings, ideas, etc., and comparing them with others previously had by him. Or again, there is no "inside world," or "something within," to the animal, while man always (at least in some degree), is aware of the "inside world," or the "something within," as distinguished from the "something without." But we must not fall into the error of supposing that the primitive man, or even the less-developed individuals of modern civilization, possess this faculty of Self Consciousness to a high degree. Many persons never have more than a misty idea of such a mental attitude. They always take themselves for granted, and never turn the gaze inward.

In some cases the fuller dawn of Self Consciousness is accompanied by a newly developed bashfulness, shyness, or that more or less morbid stale known by the common name "self-consciousness." With the faculty of introspection there often comes the tendency to employ the same too freely, and thus to become morbid, on the one hand, or else foolishly egotistical and conceited on the other hand. And this self-conscious stage is painful to many. Many find themselves entangled in a mass of mental states which one thinks is himself, or inextricably bound up with himself, and the struggle between the awakening ego and its confining sheaths is very painful in some cases. And this becomes more painful as the individual advances in Self Consciousness and nears the end at which he is to find deliverance. Man pays dearly for the gift of Self Consciousness—yet it is worth it all, for finally he reaches heights of higher consciousness and is delivered from his burden of ignorance. He pays a constantly increasing price as he advances into the territory of conscious existence and experience. The more he knows, the more he desires; and the more he desires, the more does he suffer from the pain of not having. Capacity for pain is the price man pays for his advance in the scale; but he has a corresponding capacity for pleasure accompanying it. He has not only the pain of unsatisfied desires for possession of material things, and physical wants, but also the pain arising from the lack of intelligent answers to the ever-increasing volume of problems presenting themselves for solution by his evolving intellect, and he also has pain of unsatisfied longings, disappointments, frustrated aims and ambitions, and all the rest of the list.

As man progresses, his wants multiply and his pain increases. Civilization becomes more and more complex, and new wants and lacks manifest themselves. His intelligence often fails to lead him upward, too often merely enables him to invent new and subtle means and ways of gratifying his senses in a way impossible to the animals or primitive man. Some men make a religion of the gratification of their sensuality and their appetites, and sink below the level of the beasts in this respect. Others become vain, conceited and filled with an inflated sense of the importance of their time analyzing and dissecting their moods, feelings and motives. Others exhaust their capacity for pleasure and happiness, by looking outside of themselves for happiness instead of within. These are the dark shadows cast by the light of Human Consciousness, however—the Shadows always found as the "opposite" of all real evolutionary progress.

As man progresses in the scale of Self Consciousness he begins to realize that there is an "I am" within his being to which all the feelings, the emotions, the desires, and even the thoughts and ideas are but incidents. In this high stage he perceives himself to be an "I am" surrounded by his mental and emotional tools and belongings—a Sun surrounded by its whirling worlds and activities. He realizes that the Ego is not only superior to the body, but also to the feelings; and he learns now not only how to master and intelligently use his body, but also how to intelligently master and use his intellect and his emotions.

If we are willing to believe in this mastery over the body, we must be prepared to believe in the mastery over our own inner thoughts and feelings. That a man should be a prey to any thought that chances to take possession of his mind is commonly among us assumed as unavoidable. It may be a matter of regret that he should be kept awake all night from anxiety as to the solution of some business problem on the morrow, but that he should have the power of determining whether he should be kept awake or not seems an extravagant demand. Once the matter is fairly understood, it should be as easy to expel an obnoxious thought from the mind as it is to shake a stone out of your shoe; and until a man can do that it is just nonsense to talk about his ascendancy over Nature, and all the rest of it.

As a well known writer says:

> It is one of the most promising doctrines of certain schools of thought that the power of expelling thoughts or, if need be, killing them dead on the spot, must be attained. Naturally the art requires practice, but like other arts, when once acquired there is no mystery or difficulty about it. And it is worth the practice. It may fairly be said that life only begins when this art has been acquired. For obviously, when, instead of being ruled by individual thought, the whole flock of them in their immense multitude and variety and capacity is ours to direct and dispatch and employ where we list, life becomes a thing so vast and grand compared with what it was before that its former condition may well appear almost antenatal. If you can kill a thought dead for the time being you can do anything with it that you please. And therefore it is that this power is so valuable. And it not only frees a man from mental torment (which is nine-tenths at least of the torments of life), but it gives to him a concentrated power of handling mental work absolutely unknown to him before.[032]

How to Kill Worry

While at work your thought is to be actually concentrated on it, undistracted by anything whatever irrelevant to the matter in hand—pounding away like a great engine with giant power and perfect economy—no wear and tear of friction or dislocation of parts owing to the working of different forces at the same time. When the work is finished, if there is no more occasion for the use of the machine it must stop equally, absolutely—stop entirely; no worrying; and a man must retire into that region of his consciousness where his free self dwells. I say that the power of

---

032   Found in *The Secret Doctrine of the Rosicrucians* (1918) and also attributed to "a well known writer."

the thought-machine itself is enormously increased by the difficulty of letting it alone on the one hand, and of using it singly and with concentration the other. It becomes a true tool, which the master-workman lays down when done with, but which only a bungler carries about with him all the time to show that he is the possessor of it.

If the reader will master the idea expressed here he will become a Master of Mind. And he will extend the idea to the field of his Emotions, and will put into practice there the idea and method, he will also become a Master of his Emotions—an accomplishment of inestimable value. But before doing either of these things he will find it necessary to come to a full realization of the fact that his Self—his real "I"—something superior to and transcending both his thought and his emotions. He must enter into a vivid realization of the "I am" before he may be able to "I do" regarding these accomplishments.

When the "I" knows itself to be Self and Master, then only is it able to take its throne and enforce its Will upon its subjects in the world of its thoughts, desires, feelings and emotions.

Not only may the enlightened ego manifest its power along the lines above indicated, but it may also work its will in that region which is called "The Subconscious Mind." The latter is merely that great region of mind outside of the limits of the concentrated field of attention. In that great region a great part of the thinking of the average man is performed, the results being flashed into the field of his attention in a more or less haphazard way.

The man who has grasped the reality and power of the "I" or the "ego" is able to issue positive commands to this part of his mental machinery and not only cause it to perform the work of thought classification, induction and deduction for him, but also to present the report of such work to his conscious attention at any specified time and place. The Masters of Mind relieve themselves of much of the drudgery of ordinary intellectual processes in this way and obtain results logically perfect and ready for use according to the measure of training and direction which they have been able to impose upon the aforesaid regions of their mind.

There are wonderful regions in the Higher Planes of Consciousness, awaiting the exploration of the wise of the race, and the Enlightened Egos of the future may reach heights of mental achievement which are so far above those dreamed of by the average person of the race as to appear like the wildest fiction.

Ego Consciousness is the essence of wisdom, happiness and life and Cosmic Consciousness is the quintessence of evolution and the Eternal Verities.

The Sermon on the Mount
For Subtermen and Christians
St. Matthew, Chapter 5

And seeing the multitudes, He went up into a mountain: and when He was set, His disciples came unto Him:

And He opened His mouth, and taught them, saying,

Blessed are the poor in spirit: for theirs is the Kingdom of Heaven.

Blessed are they that mourn: for they shall be comforted.

Blessed are the meek: for they shall inherit the Earth.

Blessed are they which do hunger and thirst after righteousness: for they shall be filled.

Blessed are the merciful: for they shall obtain mercy.

Blessed are the pure in heart: for they shall see God.

Blessed are the peace-makers: for they shall be called the Children of God.

Blessed are they which are persecuted for righteousness' sake: for theirs is the Kingdom of Heaven.

Blessed are ye, when men shall revile you, and persecute you, and shall say all manner of evil against you falsely, for My sake.

Rejoice, and be exceeding glad: for great is your reward in Heaven: for so persecuted they the prophets which were before you.

Think not that I am come to destroy the law, or the prophets: I am not come to destroy, but to fulfill.

For verily I say unto you, till heaven and earth pass, one jot or one tittle shall in no wise pass from the law, till all be fulfilled.

The Gospel According to Malfew Seklew

The Sermon on the Mountain
For Supercrats and Supermanitarians

Blessed are the rich in spirit, for theirs is the Kingdom of Knowledge in a world of wisdom, wealth and health.

Blessed are they that rejoice and are glad, for they shall be comforted by laughter which is the juice of joy, the thief of grief, the foe of woe, and the masterpiece of merriment.

Blessed are the strong, for they shall inherit the Earth and the fullness thereof.

Blessed are they which do hunger and thirst after wisdom, for they shall be filled with happiness, hope and self-realization.

Blessed are the tolerant and the tactful for they shall obtain the peace that passeth all misunderstanding.

Blessed are the pure in thought, for they shall see themselves as they are.

Blessed are the pacemakers, for they shall be called the Children of Cosmic Consciousness.

Blessed are they who fight for righteousness' sake, for theirs is the Crown of Consciousness.

Blessed are you when men shall understand you and support you and say all manner of good of you—for their own sakes.

Rejoice and be exceeding glad, for great is your reward in being—yourself. You shall live in your own Heaven while you are on Earth; and so live that others may see your good works and glorify your faith in yourself and in humanity. For verily I say unto you, I am not come to destroy, but to fulfill the Laws of Nature, which when obeyed bring health, wealth and happiness to all. Consciousness is the essence of life.

Egoism is the Law of the Ego
The Seven Laws that Dominate Mankind

1. The first law of human Nature is Self-Realization, which is the great urge for Happiness. The fact that pioneers, martyrs and suicides die to realize themselves, is proof sufficient that self-preservations is not the first law of Nature.
2. The second law of human Nature is self-preservation, which expresses the Will-to-Live.
3. The third law of human Nature is procreation, which expresses the Will-to-Pleasure. To get and beget is Nature's demand to mankind.
4. The fourth law of human Nature is exploitation, which demonstrates the Will-to-Power. This law is also the first law of individual and industrial progress.
5. The fifth law of human Nature is gregariousness. Inferior human beings group through fear and for warmth and self-love.
6. The sixth law of human Nature is co-operation. Intelligent human beings group together for mutual aid and to increase their power, for co-operation is the first law of weakness.
7. The seventh law of human Nature is socialization. Superior organisms group together to increase their happiness and to preserve and perpetuate their power and personalities.

• • •

All exertion and struggle in human history, all aspirations and researches of science find their common aim in the freedom of man—in the subjection of Nature to the sway of his mind.

Natural Laws Have No Pity.

The Seven Wonders of the Ego, or the Seven Psychic Sensations

The March of Man from Nebulosity to Knowledge,
from Unconsciousness of Condition to Consciousness of Self
—to Enlightened Egoism.
The Seven Points of Progress.
The Seven Concepts of Consciousness.
A Revelation of Revaluations.

From a Psychological Standpoint:

Simpoleon

A mass of matter that does not matter much, except when exploited. He travels along the line of least resistance looking for work, and finds slavery. He can see as far into the future as the eye of a potato can peer into the past. He ambles through space with the courage of a carrot; the culture of a cucumber; the consciousness of a cauliflower; the caution of a cabbage; the turpitude of a turnip; the rapacity of a radish; the ferocity of a fig; the pluck of a prune; the punch of a parsnip; the perspicacity of a pineapple; the pertinacity of a peach; the pugnacity of a pear; and the psychology of a sundowner in the swamps of self-pity, in the depths of despair.

Hopeoleon

One whose chief dope is hope. He suffers from inflammation of the imagination and costiveness of conception. He accepts what he doesn't understand, and advocates that which he cannot comprehend. He knows as much about human Nature as a profiteer knows about the perfumes of Paradise.

Demoleon

A semi-sane, hemi-hatched and demi-developed organism afflicted with bowlegged beliefs, knock-kneed notions and bifurcated opinions. He suffers from democratic delusions—is an ego on the half-shell.

Psycholeon

One who stands on the threshold of thought, in the throes of thought, struggling to escape from the 6,000 delusions, illusions and confused conclusions which burden the brain of mankind. He gazes into the eyeball of ecstasy without getting dizzy with delight whenever he murders the Microbe of Misery or assassinates the Atom of Agony.

Aristopeon

One who recognizes that whatever is, is right, until necessity demands a change. He accepts the fact that all progress is Aristocratic and never democratic; that it is original, aboriginal and always individual—not social.

An Aristopeon is a Gladiator of Gladness, a Surgeon of Shallow Selfishness, a Slaughterer of Stale Shibboleths and False Formulas, a Dissector of Desire, and a Manufacturer of Moods and Methods.

Egocrat

One who can mould his environment to his own desires. A conscious Egoist with psychological powers which enable him to vivisect vices, virtues, vanities and vibrations. He can audit his own agonies, minimize misery, mortify malice, manufacture mirth, pulverize piffle and paralyze his own paralogies.

An Egocrat is one who handles the Biological Imperatives with ease and elegance; he is a messenger of mercy and manufactures mirth until the juice of joy comes from every pregnant pore galore, with an encore and some more.

A conscious egoist who assists the Electron of Ecstacy to assassinate the microbe of misery without mercy and mortification of motive.

Supercrat

A first cousin to the Superman, who heralds the coming of Supermanity. He can peer with security into the futurity, sum up your history with art and sapidity, clean up a mystery with ease and rapidity, and give an opinion with force and lucidity; with marvelous amity he overcometh calamity, and void of all shamity and don't care a damity, he changes organity with an urbanity minus profanity that startles humanity. With psychic sagacity he expresses himself on matters that matter. With dynamic capacity he extols poor humanity, with mental audacity he explains supermanity, with singular sanity, regardless of what you may think of his vanity, oft driving his foes to the verge of insanity, or making them cling to the roots of reality. For he is the very model of a modern man material, who teaches Mentoidology in private and in serial. With globules of gladness he fills your mind full of mirth, offering them to you for what they are worth, as he dashes through space ere he falls off the earth.

A Supercrat is one who has acquired the art of socializing his own selfishness and distributes with discretion and distinction the surplus value of his own ego.

The Supercrat is a disillusioned ego: a new-laid ego void of chimerical conceptions and heavenly hallucinations, without delusions, political, social, sexual, civil, ethical, religious or economic; with hedonistic proclivities and libertarian ideals, propagating economics without agony, politics without tears, and sociology without a sob.

Such is this ego who defies the community
With power and impunity,
And makes no apology
For rushing the race,
In the Cosmic chase;
And winning the race
With a smile on his face.
So take all these elements,
All that are fusible;
Melt them all down in pitkin or crucible,
Set them to simmer and take off the scum.
And a Supercratic Ego is the *residuum*.

Quotations

"To envy anybody is to confess one's self his inferior."[033]
—Julie De Lespenasse.

"I am convinced that the most dangerous animal on earth is that insane animal, the moralistic man."
—Tak Kak.

"I have been a selfish being all my life in practice, though not in theory."[034]
—Jane Austen.

"There's something bed-rock in complacent selfishness which nothing can wear away."[035]
—H. Walpole.

"How true it is that Providence arranges / That human Nature never, never changes."
—A. A. M.

"Man is Naturally innocent, timid, stupid, and vain."
—Mandeville.

"Mighty is he who conquers himself."[036]
—Lao Tzu.

---

033   Julie-Jeanne-Éléonore de Lespinasse (1732 - 1776). Salon-holder. It's possible Malfew sourced this quote from *A Thousand Flashes of French Wit, Wisdom and Madness*, by J. de Finod (1902).
034   Jane Austen (1775 - 1817). Author. Quote from *Pride and Prejudice*.
035   Hugh Walpole (1884 - 1941). Author. Quote from *Harmer John* (1926).
036   Lao Tzu. Founder of Taoism. Quote from *The Sayings of Lao-Tzu*, (Lionel Giles translation 1905).

The Seven Lines of Demarcation

1st. Man learns from studying himself from the biological standpoint that: He is not descended from the angels, but that he has ascended from the lower forms of life. Not an angel out of a job, but a human being looking for work or happiness.

2nd. From a deterministic standpoint he learns that: Man is the creature of his environment; the slave of circumstances, as an unconscious ego, but when he awakens to the consciousness of his own potentialities, he can become the engineer of his environment, and the operator of his own opportunities.

3rd. From a governmental standpoint: Man learns that governments are built on hope and kept alive by taxation; that government makes laws to suit the interests of those who govern, and compel the interest of the governed.

4th. From a moral standpoint: Man finds out that moralities are made to suit the interests of those who govern and to pacify those who perceive the power of truth, and who know that Society is built on the patience of the poor. That the only sin is ignorance.

5th. From an economic standpoint: Man learns that economic power is the one thing needful. Property is power. Where property resides personality presides.

6th. From an Egoistic standpoint: Man learns that egoism is everything, for everything is caustic; that the Ego is the centre of sensation and evolution; that man lives to satisfy his chief desire and that self-realization is the first law of his life.

The Gospel According to Malfew Seklew

7th. From a Psychic standpoint: Man learns that a recognition of these forces plus an understanding of the power of mind over matter and mortals, and a knowledge of how to cultivate the will to power, makes him a conscious Ego. An Ego means you or I, *viz*: a distinct personality, a reality, an individuality. An Ego is the centre of sensation, the sum total of all impressions, impingements and sensations registered on the sensorium and realized in memory.

The Thirteen Affirmations

1. That Selfishness is the Supreme Law.
2. That Egoism is the Law of Life.
3. That Self-love is the only love that never dies.
4. That Self-interest, not Love, rules the world.
5. That the twin enemies of mankind are Ignorance and Crude Selfishness.
6. The Biological Imperatives are: To get and beget and to fight.
7. The Categorical Imperatives are: The Will to Live, the Will to Pleasure, and the Will to Power.
8. The Psychological Imperatives: are Self-knowledge, Self-control and Self-realization.
9. The Eternal Verities are: Selfishness; Vanity, Hate and Love.
10. The Missing Link in Evolution is the Ego Conscious organism—an Ego who has found himself out—from within, because he understands things from without.
11. The Missing Link in Progress is the Will-to-Power man—the Plus-man of the period—the Great Exploiter—who is the Elbow Grease of Evolution and the Great Benefactor.
12. The Missing Link in Civilization is the Social Supercrat who gives away the surplus value of his Ego with discretion, dignity and benignity.
13. The Riddle of the Universe has been solved by the Supercrat who has found out that he is the center of sensations; a microcosm in a macrocosm, who has become aware of his own possibilities and potentialities, and thus becomes the Factor of his own Future; the Masterpiece of Mood, Method and Mentality the Director of his own Destiny, and the Manufacturer of his own Millenium to order—without disorder.

The Thirteen Commandments

1. Thou shalt be true to the Earth and Thyself.
2. Thou shalt have no other god than Thyself.
3. Thou shalt find thyself out, from within, and become a Conscious Egoist.
4. Thou shalt cultivate thy Social Instinct until thou becomes a Social Supercrat.
5. Thou shalt quicken evolution by conscious endeavor.
6. Thou shalt proclaim that Enlightened Selfishness, only, can save mankind from sin and suffering.
7. Thou shalt take the Tool of Thought, the greatest tool in the world, and prove that the heart of the world may be all right, but its head seems to be all wrong.
8. Thou shalt co-operate with Congenial Atoms and help to make Millenniums to order—without disorder.
9. Thou shalt appreciate Master-Morality and depreciate slave-morality.
10. Thou shalt affirm that vanity is not a vice, but a virtue.
11. Thou shalt socialize thy selfishness and preach the new Dispensation of gladness, wisdom and power.
12. Thou shalt develop thy surplus value of thine own ego and give it away with pride and pleasure.
13. Thou shalt "sow a thought and reap an action; sow an action and reap a habit; sow a habit and reap a character; sow a character and reap a destiny."[037]

> "To be what we are, and to become what we are capable of becoming, is the only end of life."[038]
>
> —R. L. Stevenson.

---

037   Swami Sivananda Saraswati (1887 - 1963). Hindu teacher.
038   Robert Louis Stevenson (1850 - 1894). Author. Quote from *Familiar Studies of Men and Books* (1882).

The Thirteen Problems

The following will be readily solved when ignorance and crude selfishness are replaced by wisdom and enlightened selfishness controlled by the Social Supercrat:

1. The problem of Democracy.
2. The problem of Distribution.
3. The problem of Poverty.
4. The problem of Labor.
5. The problem of Employment.
6. The problem of War.
7. The problem of Religion.
8. The problem of Diet.
9. The problem of Prostitution.
10. The problem of Birth Control.
11. The problem of Divorce.
12. The problems of Morality and Education.
13. The problem of a Sinful Civilization.

Enlightened selfishness will abolish sin, for sin is simply ignorance running riot in the realm of raw realities. As super consciousness increases in the minds of men, sin decreases, for the Conscious Egoist uses his newly acquired wisdom to destroy those things which tend to impede his progress, and to increase the number of things that tend to help and improve him. The result is a higher civilization. Sin is an ecclesiastical crime, and when properly understood it will found to be an invention of the clergy, to enable them to better control a credulous laity.

> "The problem of Democracy is solved as soon as the people learn the truth about Democracy, *viz*: Why Democracy is the only mother that is ashamed of her children."[039]
>
> —Lord Balfour.

The problem of Distribution is solved as soon as man learns how to socialize his selfishness and distribute the surplus value of his Ego with pleasure and profit to himself.

The problem of Poverty will be solved as soon as the Government realizes that it will be to the interest of all if every poor family is given three acres of land and taught the science of intensive cultivation of the soil. This scheme, if carried out and accompanied by free advice on birth control, would soon extirpate poverty from the land.

The problem of Labor will be solved as soon as the workers learn how to use their own labor power for their own benefit and become self-employers.

The problem of Unemployment can be solved by the Trade Unions taking care of their own unemployed as follows: Buy as much land, which can be used for the raising of foodstuffs to be used by the unemployed until there is a demand for their services. This land is to be tilled and cultivated by experts, assisted by the unemployed so as to produce the greatest possible return for the least expenditure of energy and money.

The problem of War will be solved when we understand what John Ruskin said:

> War hath its victories no less renowned than peace. All the pure and noble arts of peace are founded on war; no great art ever yet rose on earth, but among a nation of soldiers... The common notion that peace and the virtues of civil life flourished together I found to be wholly untenable. Peace and the vices of civil life only flourish together. We talk of peace and learning, of

---

039   Earl Arthur James Balfour (1848 - 1930). Prime Minister of the United Kingdom 1902 - 1905.

peace and plenty, of peace and civilization; but I have found that those were not the words which the Muse of History coupled together; that, on her lips, the words were: peace and sensuality, peace and selfishness, peace and corruption, peace and death. I found that all the great nations learned their truth of word, and strength of were nourished in war and wasted by peace; taught by war and deceived by peace: trained by war and betrayed by peace—in a word they were born in war and expired in peace. [040]

War is biological necessity: for it preserves the fighting spirit in man.

War is the ransom paid by humanity for progress.

War may be waste, but waste is better than disgrace.

The war of opinion is everlasting, as is the war of Will.

The problem of Religion will be solved when man becomes wise enough to be his own god.

The problem of Diet will be solved as soon as human beings learn the true value of foodstuffs and cease eating adulterated food.

The problem of Prostitution can be solved by abolishing all laws against the Natural right of every individual to exercise his or her sexual functions, regardful of reason and Natural law.

The problem of Birth Control can be solved by giving free advice to all on this important phase of life, as they do in Holland, with the aid and consent of the Government.

The problem of Divorce can be solved by making trial marriages fashionable and legal.

The problems of Morality and Education are solved as soon as the individual is told the truth from an Egoistic and Natural Moral standpoint instead of from an Altruistic and pseudo-moral standpoint.

The problem of a Sinful Civilization is solved when the peo-

---

040   John Ruskin (1819 - 1900), art critic. Quote is an inversion of a quote from John Milton, "Sonnett: To the Lord General Cromwell" (1652).

ple are convinced that there is no sin but ignorance, and that all life must be understood from an Egoistic basis before a real Civilization is possible.

Trinities that Mould Mankind

"The language of Nature is not understood because it is too simple."[041]

— Schopenhauer.

"Lo! To my own Gods I go / Perhaps they will give me greater ease / Than your cold Christ and tangled trinities." [042]

— Rudyard Kipling.

"Thought is mind-stuff in motion."[043]

The Three Laws of Thought
1. The Law of Identity. Whatever is, is.
2. The Law of Contradiction. Nothing can both be, and not be.
3. The Law of Excluded Middle. Everything must either be, or not be.

Three Manifestations of Mentality
A true sense of proportion and comparison.

The art of compromise.

A true spirit of Justice.

These three forces, when in operation, are evidences of a real civilization.

"There are three substances," says Descartes, "God, Thought and Matter."[044]

A great thinker passes through three stages of apotheosis; first a heretic, next a prophet, then an institution.

"I wish, I can, I will—these are the three trumpet notes to victory."[045]

---

041 Arthur Schopenhauer (1788 - 1860). Philosopher.
042 Joseph Rudyard Kipling (1865 - 1936). Author. Quote is from a poem found in the chapter heading of "Lispeth," from the book *Plain Tales from the Hills*. It reads: "To my own Gods I go. / It may be they shall give me greater ease / Than your cold Christ and tangled Trinities." and is attributed to "The Convert."
043 William Kingdon Clifford (1845 - 1879). Philosopher. Coined the phrase "mind-stuff" in "On the Nature of Things-in-Themselves" for *Mind*, Vol. 3, No. 9 (1878). *Mind* was a magazine that published positive reviews of egoist authors.
044 René Descartes (1596 - 1650). Philosopher. Quote found in *Thinkers and Thinking* by James Edmund Garretso (1873) and *The Laws of Heredity* by George Williamson (1887).
045 Anonymous. *Râja Yoga Messenger*, Vol. XVII No. 1. (1921).

The Trinity of Growth

Instinct, Intuition and Reason. Instinct preserved and perpetuated man until intuition came to lift him upward towards Reason. Reason rescued him from ignorance and greed, and low grade selfishness.

Instinct is thought that has become a habit; intuition is unconscious thought, and reason is conscious thought. The rudder of reason is the Regulator of Righteousness.

The Trinity of Natural Wealth

The Earth, the Sun, the Sea. The basic industries on which all other industry, all business of every kind, all human life for that matter, depend, are those which extract the raw material of industry from these reservoirs.

The Trinity of Surplus Value

Capital is the oil of production.

Capitalists are the Engineers of production.

Capitalism is the science of co-operation and mass production—the trinity from which all progress, enlightenment and wealth emanates.

The Worker's Trinity

Toil—the workers toil for wages.

Turmoil—is wrought by strikes and lockouts.

Tribulation—begins when wages end:

No work—No wages—No happiness.

The Trinity of Happiness

The Will to Live; the Will to Pleasure; the Will to Power. All men have the Will to Live; many the Will to Pleasure, but few possess the Will to Power.

The Trinity of Wisdom

Psychic Sagacity, Dynamic Capacity and Perspicacious Pugnacity.

Psychic Sagacity is the essence of foresight, hindsight, and insight.

Dynamic Capacity is the energy of endurance.

Perspicacious Pugnacity is the fighting spirit, which is the Will-to-win.

The Trinity of Ease

Treasure, Leisure and Pleasure.

Treasure is necessary before leisure is possible.

Leisure is necessary before pleasure is permissible.

The highest form of pleasure is found in the cultivation of art, literature, science and other adornments of leisured life.

The Trinity of Power

Wish, Desire and Will.

A wish is the beginning of desire; desire is the dynamo of doing, and will is the engineer of success.

The Trinity of Self-gratification

Vanity, Hate and Love.

Vanity is external; hate infernal, and love internal and local.

The Trinity of Knowledge

Subconsciousness, Consciousness and Superconsciousness.

Subconsciousness is our subjective self and the seat of memory; Consciousness is our objective self and the seat of emotions; Superconsciousness is the art of analyzing self from all angles.

The Trinity of Thought

Self-Knowledge, Self-Control and Self-Respect.

Self-Knowledge is necessary before Self-Control is mastered, and Self-Control commands Self-Respect.

The Trinity of Self-Interest

Prejudice, Conceit and Calculation.

Prejudice is self-love, founded on Conceit, and Conceit is calculated to look after Self-Interest.

Trinity of Life

Self-preservation, Self-analyzation and Self-Realization, the three avenues to the higher life.

The Trinity of Hope

Health, Wealth and Happiness

We need health to enable us to get wealth, and wealth is useful in the pursuit of happiness, when judiciously expended.

The Trinity of Consummation

Inspiration, Aspiration and Self-Realization.

The Trinity of Illumination

Intuition, Initiation and Imagination.

The Trinity of Expectation

Instinct, Imitation and Initiation.

Trinity of the Mind

Thought, Imagination and Will is the great Trinity of the Mind. Thought is the regulator, Imagination is the illuminator, and Will is the dictator of the Mind. The tool of Thought is the greatest implement of the intellect, and the greatest tool in the world. It is seldom used, except by the psychologists, who were the first to use it and develop it to its present dimensions. Mind is the magic power that moves and makes all things.

The Trinity of Religions

Paganism, the Religion of Force; Christianity, the Religion of Service; Superology, the Religion of Will and Power.

The pugnacity of Puritanism made it powerful. The violence of its virtue made it feared, and the morbidity of its morality made it mad and sad.

Three Great Emotions

Love, Hate and Fear.

No man ever does anything unless he is driven by one or more of these three great emotions. Choose which emotion you will obey and thus avoid confusion of thought and action.

The Trinity of Locksmiths

"The human mind has three keys opening all locks: Knowledge, Reflection and Imagination. In these three things everything is contained."[046]

—Victor Hugo.

The Trinity of Genius

Initiation, Imagination and Inspiration.

What is Genius?

The genius performs his benefits for mankind because he is obliged to do so and cannot do otherwise. It is an instinct organically inherent in him which he is obeying. He would suffer if he did not obey its impulse. That the

046   Victor Marie Hugo (1802 - 1885). Poet. Quote from *The Press*, Volume LIII, No. 15844 (1917). This is one of a number of quotes from New Zealand newspapers, probably obtained from Arthur Desmond, aka "Ragnar Redbeard."

average masses will benefit by it does not decide the matter for him. Men of genius must find their sole reward in the fact that thinking, acting, originating, they live out their higher qualities and thus become conscious of their originality, to the accompaniment of powerful sensations of pleasure. There is no other satisfaction for the most sublime genius, as well as the lowest living being swimming in its nourishing fluid, than the sensation, as intensive as possible, of its own Ego.[047]

—Nordau.

Genius is the inborn faculty of knowing how to do a thing without knowing how it's done—until it's done.

"The present (genius) which is made to some of us at our birth is not that same thing which the others can acquire, by study, by thought, and by time."[048]

—Jean Ingelow.

Genius instinctively knows what lesser minds must needs be taught. The atmosphere in which genius moves calls forth his creations.

Shakespeare was never taught the principles of dramatic art; Bach had an instinctive appreciation of the laws of harmony, and Turner had some insight into the laws of painting—they simply looked—and understood.

Life is a Trinity: Become, Beget, Begone. The greatest of the Trinities—Selfishness, Vanity and Hate—tortures, torments and tantalizes mankind so long as man is unconscious of himself. It is the Trinity of Malevolence; but it will be the Trinity of Benevolence when man understands how to socialize his selfishness, sanitize his vanity, and regulate his hate.

---

047   Max Simon Nordau (1849 - 1923). Zionist. Quote from *The Eagle and the Serpent* No. 18, which in turn quotes from "Paradoxes" by Nordau (1896).
048   Jean Ingelow (1820 - 1897). Poet. As quoted in *Writing the Short Story* by J. Berg Esenwein (1919).

The Trinity of Emotion

Passion, Pain and Pleasure.

The Trinity of Motion

Love, Life and Laughter.

The Trinity of Uplift

Egoism, Altruism and Socialism.

  The three Great Fatalities are Hunger, Fear and Ignorance.

Catechism of Consciousness

What is Personality?

The outward expression of a strong individuality, an Ego with a vision.

Personality: The word may be defined as the capital "I" in I-dentity, the irrepressible Ego.

The man with personality, while he is an Egoist, is not necessarily an Egotist. (An Egotist is a boastful Egoist.) Personality has always counted tremendously both in culture and conduct. It counts today more than ever because it walks hand in hand with publicity. A man or woman with personality is never a type. He imposes himself upon others because he is different from them; he exudes from every pore of his skin a sort of "force;" he is above convention and tradition, although he may use both to achieve his ends. Really, he is the acme of self-expression, and his self-expression is almost immeasurable.

Personalities made to order: There are eight executives in our bodies who control the actions of our bodies. Their names are: The Pituitary gland, Adrenal gland, Pineal gland, Thyroid gland, the Thymus, the Pancreas, the Gonads, the Parathyroids.

Now that Science understands the functions of these glands, personalities can be made to order by changing the degree of activity of the glands according to the needs of the individual.

What is Individuality?

The inward manifestation of a unique Ego who uses the tool of thought.

What is Psychology?

Psychology originally meant the study of the Soul.

The human soul was thought to be a sort of entity, exhibiting qualities or faculties which became manifest to us as various psychological manifestations.

The last century saw the gradual development of a psychology without a soul—a psychology based upon the study of mind as manifested in human beings; it therefore became the study of consciousness.

Psychology is the precursor of all progress, or Curiosity crowned with Consciousness. Psychology discovers, Philosophy uncovers and Science recovers. In other words: Psychology perceives, Philosophy conceives, and Science receives.

Philosophy is the first born of Psychology; Science is the offspring of Philosophy.

Psychology is the science of the mind; Philosophy the science of thought, and Science the philosophy of things.

The world is the marble,

Your mind is the sculptor,

Your thought is the chisel.

What is Mind?

The first expression of mind is instinct, then, intuition, imagination, inspiration, and aspiration, thus bringing forth supreme consciousness. Mind pervades the universe. It transcends every individual; it inspires; it creates and actualizes infinite realities.

Mind is the matrix of matter and matter is mind that is behind the times, or mind is matter that knows its own mind.

Mind is the miracle of motion, and the monarch of mode, mood, method, and manners.

Mind is the *rendezvous* of reason,

Mind is matter in motion.

Emotion is mind in commotion and finds its apex in devotion.

Mind is the mightiest force in the world. It guides the pen of the philosopher and the sword of the warrior and the hand of the aristocrat and the producer. It is the highest expression of egoistic energy known to mankind. It was the last portion of man to be developed and is the least understood. It is the most important part of man and yet we are only just beginning to study its laws.

What is Consciousness?

The essence of the Ego and of life.

Consciousness is the product of inductive thought, and is the irresistible and limitless vehicle of the desires and will of mankind.

There are three Consciousnesses: The Subconsciousness, Consciousness, and Superconsciousness.

Subconsciousness seeks to preserve the Ego.

Consciousness seeks to please the Ego.

Superconsciousness seeks to improve the Ego.

Subconsciousness expresses the will to live.

Consciousness expresses the will to pleasure.

Superconsciousness expresses the will to power.

These are the first glimpses of the real issues of life, which bring us to the first principle of life, Egoism.

What is Conscience?

Conscience is the Conservatory of crude concepts and the depot of delusions.

Conscience is a torture chamber invented by the dead to torture the living.

Conscience must be crucified on the cross of Consciousness before the Ego can be emancipated from false formulas, stale shibboleths, and mildewed moralisms.

What is Civilization?

It is localization.

The application of mind to the problems of life.

> "All human activities, all social phenomena are rigidly subject to the Natural law."[049]
>
> —Lester Ward.

What is the Soul?

The Egoistic definition is: The Soul of man is the Ego; for the Ego is the totality of things.

What is an Ego?

An individual, who may be either a nonentity or a personality with a punch.

What is Man?

An entity with an identity.

"Man," says Socrates, "is the measure of all things; yet he is an Ego within an Ego, a universal."[050] A part may not act in itself, but only as a whole. Mind is the immortal part of being, capable of existing after its connection with the body is served. It is made up of certain faculties, reason, memory, etc.

Man is of slow growth. The best of him—the brain—was the last part of him to be developed; the best part of his brain—the mind—was the last part of his brain to be developed; the best of his mind—consciousness—was the last part of his mind to be discovered; the best part of his consciousness—will—was the last part of his consciousness to be utilized; the best part of will is the power to will, which develops the Will to Power.

---

049   Lester Frank Ward (1841 - 1913). Sociologist. Quote from *The Psychic Factors of Civilization* (1893): "Nothing was more natural than the generalization that the acts of adults do not differ generically from those of children, and the wider generalization that all human activies and all social phenomena are as rigidly subject to natural law as are the activities of children and animals and the movements of terrestrial and celestial bodies, was but an additional short step."

050   Protagoras (c490 BC - c420 BC). Philosopher. Claimed man is the measure of all things.

What is Life?

Just one thing after another. To become, beget, begone, or to get, beget, and sometimes reflect.

To satisfy the dominant desire of the moment and to be filled with self-fullness.

What is the purpose of Life?

To pursue pleasure and avoid pain. Man loves to wallow in the pleasures of the palate, the pleasures of the pelvic region, and, when he is intellectual, in the pleasures of memory.

Life's punctuation: Infancy, notes of admiration; youth, interrogation; manhood, dashes; old age, full stops.

> "Life is short, art long, opportunity fleeting, experiment uncertain, and judgment difficult."[051]
>
> —Hippocrates.

> Life is a weary interlude -
> Which doth short joys, long woes include;
> The world the stage, the prologue tears;
> The acts vain hopes and varied fears;
> The scene shifts up with loss of breath,
> And leaves no epilogue, but death.[052]
>
> —Bishop King.

What is Human Nature?

Human Nature is a compound of impingements, impressions, instincts, intuitions, imaginations, inspirations, and aspirations—plus the Trinity of Power: Selfishness, Vanity and Hate; and the Trinity of Triumph: The Will to Live, the Will to Pleasure, and the Will to Power.

> Human Nature in the most remote huts under the northern lights is identical to that which exists in the thatched shacks that girdle the globe at the equator. Birth, life, death—these

---

051   Hippocrates (c460 BC - 377 BC). Philosopher. Quote from *Aphorisms*.
052   Quote from *Treasury of Wisdom, Wit and Humor, Odd Comparisons and Proverbs* (1891).

are the same everywhere, in palace or in kraal. Love, hatred, jealousy, ambition, hunger, remorse, hope, pity, cruelty, kindness, hospitality, pride, envy superstition, fear, shyness, greed, satiety, cowardice, bravery—all these things are common to all men. They came with us from the womb and they go with us to the tomb, basically alike in their origins and causes, in their manifestations, in their effect on behavior, in their results; differing only in the minor matter of custom and geographical practicer.[053]

—S. Sutherland.

What is Memory?

The *rendezvous* of recollections, revelations, revaluations, and realizations.

What is a Reverie?

A masquerade of memories.

What is Woman?

A mystery with a history which has never been written.

Woman is the psychological factor in generation. Man germinates; woman generates—and sometimes a genius creates.

Woman, when she awakens from her long sleep, will be the Saviour of mankind. When she evolves into enough psychic sagacity to produce a Superman. When woman knows her own powers of mind, as a psychological expert, she will produce to order the genius as accurately and scientifically as she does nowadays produce the Simpoleon, or Cipher.

Wish, Desire and Will

A Wish is the beginning of a will, a Choice Concept.

A Desire is a wish intensified by determination.

A Will is concentrated desire, backed by the will to Conquer.

---

053   Sidney Sutherland. Journalist. Interview with Lillian Gish in *Liberty* magazine, July 1927.

What is Will?

Will is the essence of energy, and the 100 percent interest on individuality.

Will is the Engineer of the Ego, Epochs, Evolution, and Eternity.

Will is the majesty of motion; the miracle of method, and the masterpiece of matter and mentality.

Will is the warrior of wisdom, crowned with conquest over conscience, convention, custom, and the commonplace.

What is Self-love?

"Self-love is the love of self and of everything for the sake of self. When fortune gives the means, self-love makes men idolize themselves and tyrannize over others."[054]

—La Rouchfaucauld.

"Self-love never reigns so absolutely as in the passion of love. We are always ready to sacrifice the peace of those we adore, rather than lose the least part of our own."[055]

—La Rouchfaucauld.

What is Self-pity?

Self-pity is founded on wounded self-love. It is a slight intensified into an insult and an injury.

What is Ignorance?

Ignorance is that state of mind that results from false teaching, or lack of knowledge and intuition. Truth saves; ignorance kills. Truth frees; ignorance enslaves. To be ignorant of the life-producing truths that are free to all who will think, is to be on the sure road to physical, mental and moral ruin. To know the laws of Nature and live them intelligently is to be on the beautiful and pleasant road that leads to peace of mind and body.

---

054   Quotes from *Maxims*.
055   Quotes from *Maxims*. Found in *The Eagle and The Serpent* Volume 2 Number 1. September 1900.

What is a Subterman?

A Subterman is matter in the wrong place because his mind is in his muscles and his brain in his biceps.

A Superman is mind in the right place.

What is a Cheap Organism, or a Cipher?

An unripe Ego—an unfinished organism burdened with bifurcated opinions and hard-boiled beliefs. He often suffers from the pangs of impecuniosity, because he has not yet discovered himself.

What is Vanity?

Self-love satisfied for the time being—a virtue, not a vice.

Vanity is the self-love of an intelligent Egoist displayed with discretion. When self-love is flamboyantly exhibited, then it is the action of an Egotist—an Egoist who has lost control of himself for the moment.

Vanity is what one thinks of oneself with due consideration for others. The result of this comparison is compromise and harmony.

Conceit is what one thinks of oneself, without thought of what others may think of one, or without regard for the opinion of others.

Conceit is the outward expression of an ignorant Egotist. Both actions are found on the same motive—selfishness.

Conceit is the virtue of an ignorant Egotist; vanity is the virtue of a thoughtful Ego.

The value of Vanity: Vanity, like temper, is a very good thing to possess if we can only keep it under control. Vanity helps those who have not been blessed by Nature with charms or ability to endure their defects smilingly.

Vanity: In us, it is accompanied with an apprehension that we do over-value ourselves, hence our susceptibility to the confirmatory good opinion of others. But if each were to display openly his own feeling of superiority, quarrels would inevitably arise. The grand discovery whereby the ill consequences of this passion are avoided is politeness.

What is Wisdom?

Wisdom is Knowledge that has been certified by Experience.

What is Imagination?

Imagination is the illuminator of intellect; the microscope of mentality; the magnet of mood, and the magic lantern of the mind.

The man who has imagination has ideals; he thinks of things in new ways. Imagination is the fountainhead from which has sprung all human progress. Men of imagination have made all our great inventions, painted our great pictures, written our masterpieces of literature, established our great industries. Successful men in business, industry, the professions, indeed, in all human activities, invariably are men of powerful imagination.

"Imagination is the supreme gift of the gods, and the degree of its possession is the measure of any man's advantage over circumstances—the measure of his clutch on success."[056]

What is Desire?

The dynamo of love and life.

What is Hate?

The opposite of love; it is passion's slave, the pain of passion and the passion of pain.

What is Love?

Love is the dovetailing of desire with consummation. It is the most selfish of passions, for love unrequited is hatred ignited, because vanity has been slighted.

---

056   Quote from "Making the Ideal Real" in *The Gleaner* Volume 4 Number 11 (August 1913).

What is Happiness?

"The feeling that power increases, that resistance is overcome."[057]

—Nietzsche.

"Happiness lies in imagination, not in possession. We are made happy by obtaining not what others think desirable, but what we ourselves think so."[058]

—La Rouchfaucauld.

What is Self-sacrifice?

Self-sacrifice is catering to a prejudice in order to satisfy an ambition.

Self-sacrifice is Self-love, overflowing with emotion, regardless of reason and righteousness. Emotion is founded on sympathy. Sympathy is built on Self-pity, and Self-pity is Self-love in tears and selfishness in arrears.

Self-sacrifice, to be genuine, is to give away to another that which you need for yourself; otherwise, you are merely doing something to please yourself.

Self-sacrifice is really selfishness seeking satisfaction at the moment when it brings the most pleasure—when your moral concepts are gratified and your emotions are in a state of fermentation. Cultivate your surplus value and give away that which you can spare without feeling the loss, or give away only that which you find pleasure in giving.

Then there will be more happiness, and less envy, malice and jealousy on Earth.

But is there no genuine self-denial? Mandeville answers by a distinction: "Mortifying one passion to gratify another is very good, but it is not self-denial. Self-inflicted pain without any recompense—where is that to be found?"[059]

Did any man ever do an act to produce but remorse?

---

057   Quote from *The Antichrist* (1895).
058   Quote from *Maxims*.
059   Quote from *Moral Science: a Compendium of Ethics* by Alexander Bain (1896) in turn quoting Mandeville: "Mortifying one passion to gratify another is very common, but it is not self-denial; self-inflicted pain without any recompense - where is that to be found?"

"Self-denial is not a virtue; it is only the effect of prudence on rascality."[060]

—G. B. Shaw.

Egoism is the totality of sensations seeking satisfaction according to the tastes of the Ego.

What is Justice?

Justice is a measure of value, justified by comparison. Comparison produces a sense of proportion, and a true sense of it produces compromise and justice. Compromise is a balance of interests and Justice is a balance of power.

What is Morality?

A code of conduct that is rampant in any given locality. Like religion it is a geographical affliction.

What is Remorse?

The anguish of mind of one who has found himself out to be either a fool or a sinner.

Remorse is memory that has begun to ferment, A little reason will ease the fermentation, and the result will be peace and self-satisfaction.

Spinoza says: "Remorse is a defect rather than a virtue."[061]

What is Duty?

Duty is service for others, in preference for self; actually, to act from a sense of duty is to live up to one's concept of righteousness, which is an act of selfishness.

Duty brings its own reward—self-righteous—which is self-realization.

The dogma of Duty must be discarded, because it has a de-

---

060   George Bernard Shaw (1856 - 1950). Author. Quote from "Maxims for Revolutionists" in *Man and Superman* (1903).
061   Quote from *Story of Philosophy* (1924) by Will Durant (1885 - 1981).

moralizing influence on mankind. It is used as a moral whip to coerce crude conceptionists into action which tends to their own destruction and which redounds to the benefit of their enemies. It is a boomerang of blunders and a blight on the brain of man.

In place of duty exercise a true sense of proportion and justice will be done to all.

What is Progress?

All progress rests on just one thing and nothing else, and that is the incentive to individuals. No economic system is worth the paper on which its tenets are written that does not recognize this great factor as the basis of all human progress. It is the one thing we must preserve and encourage at any cost.

What is Capitalism?

A process of production for profit and power.

Capital directs; Labor is directed.

Capital creates wealth; Labor assists in the production of profit.

Capital makes labor valuable; Labor makes Capital more valuable.

Capital thinks before he succeeds; Labor feels before he thinks.

Both are necessary to each other. United they stand; divided they fall apart.

What is Socialism?

A moan in monotone for mercy and the millennium.

Socialism: A spasm of self-love masquerading as a sacrifice.

The sanctification of self-pity, the sublimation of a sob.

A querulous quiver from a man with a feverish liver.

A Sobolion's Soliloquy, brought on by sympathetic diarrhea.

Socialism is advocated by the Sobocracy, who seek economic salvation through fears and by tears.

What is Communism?

The chaos of thought in the center of chaos.

What is Bolshevism?

It is something antique, striving to produce something unique, with the usual result: disorder, discord and disaster.

What is a Philanthropist?

One who gives away his grief in the form of libraries and hospitals and churches.

What is a Fordanthropist?

One who gives away his joys and the surplus value of his Ego in the form of high wages, for short hours, thus enabling the workers to wear gold teeth, white collars and boiled shirts, without feeling conspicuous.

What is Truth?

"Truth: A conception of fact that cannot be depreciated by any human argument."

—H. L. Burnette.

What is Religion?

"Religion: A human consciousness of a superhuman intelligence."

—H. L. Burnette.

Religion: A yearning to get in touch with the Infinite.

The urge of vanity to be greater than it is possible to be.

The power of personality to be recognized by God.

The godhead in man urging towards consummation.

Religion is that seeking for security throughout eternity that commences at the grave; that hunt for solace here; that search for mind-tranquility which alike animates all thoughtless and crudely selfish creatures no matter where they live.

What is Theology?

"Superstition: A fear of a superhuman power."

—H. L. Burnette.

What is Superstition?

"Superstition: A fear of a superhuman power."

—H. L. Burnette.

What is Subconscious Mind?

Subconscious mind is the play of every thought in consciousness beneath the surface at the moment, since the stream is continually changing, flowing from the exchange to the center of the "primary unconscious." All that concerns us is the play of the fore-conscious which makes up our lives. Man's automatic subconsciousness being of a higher order was a later development than that of the reflex automatism of the brute, wherein the dividing line in response to stimulation is "attention."

It is in the plane of "primary unconsciousness," that of elaborate cells, the throne of the entire mind—that those creative concepts occur that are concerned with invention, imagination, poetry, and the fine arts.

> "Conscious is something unstable. It varies among different individuals, and varies according to the times. The peasant's conscience is old-fashioned, decrepit. It is between the consciences that are decrepit and those that are coming into being that party conflicts are waged."[062]
>
> —Ibsen.

"Conscience is held to be a unique and ultimate power of the mind like the feeling of Resistance, the sense of Taste, or the consciousness of Agreement. It is thought to be a gift of God to man and to be the dispenser of right and wrong regardless of the fact that morality differs according to the locality. It is a geographical condition of mind like religion."

062   Henrik Ibsen (1828 - 1906), Playwright.

What is Democracy?

"Democracy means the worship of mediocrity, and hatred of excellence. It means the impossibility of the great. How could great men submit to the indignities and indecencies of an election."[063]

—W. Durant.

"Democracy is an attempt to find an ego in the crowd: to make the individual feel he is a somebody, while all the time he is a nobody."

"There can he no perfect democracy until every citizen becomes a conscious Egoist—an intellectual Aristocrat."

"The Democracy has a hundred exuberant good qualities, and only one outstanding sin—it is undemocratic."[064]

—G. K. Chesterton.

"Democracy is a delusion and must ever be the tool of the unscrupulous because democrats delegate their personal power to others and patiently await the result—which is much different from what they expected."

"Democracy is that part of humanity that is behind the times—and in front of the future—without hope of success."

What is Fordanthropy?

Fordanthropy: the art of artifice; the science of a new soul in business; the psychology of muscle, motion, and mind in production.

Fordification in Business: How to make millions by employing the mutable many at high wages for short hours; the resurectio of labor while taking a rest from toil, turmoil and tribulation.

---

063   Will Durant (1885 - 1981). Author.
064   Gilbert Keith Chesterton, (1874 - 1936). Author. Quoted from *The Dial* Volume XLI Number 489 (November 1 1906).

What is a Smile?

The *pianissimo* of pleasure at the funeral of a frown.

What is Conceit?

Conceit is no receipt for righteousness.

What is Prohibition?

It is an imposture upon the people, conceived in iniquity, nurtured on prejudice and sustained by fraud and corruption.

"It lives on lies—until it dies."

Prohibition does not prohibit, but contributes to intemperance of speech and action, and intolerance in drinking and thinking.

The prohibitionists are extra-emotional, ultra-devotional, super-hysterical, highly-chimerical, wildly-etherical, rashly-unreasonable. When they talk about the fiend rum, they are erotic, neurotic, exotic, quixotic, chaotic, and tommyrotic in their tirades against the tyranny of drink. They have rheumatism in their reason and their morality has been inoculated with the microbe of misery.

Ask a purblind Prohibitionist to vote for the nullification of the 18th Amendment. He will certainly refuse, because his principles or his prejudice will not permit him to do so. Ask a parboiled Puritan to do something that he deems evil, even though it has been proven to be good for his fellow man, he will refuse, because his conscious would be outraged and pain would be his portion for the time being. All prohibitionists, Puritan and professional uplifters, are malicious, anti-social and meanly selfish when their pet prejudices (which they call principles) are opposed or exposed. That's the reason why we have lynching bees and tar & feather parties in the moonlight, conducted by unripe thinkers and morbid moralists.

The Puritan and the Prohibitionist are intensely cruel and malignantly selfish. To enforce their will on the world, they would make millions miserable if they could. They are enemies of happiness, freedom and progress.

The paradox is that prohibition, put over by the will of the people's representatives, is defined by the won't of the people themselves.

• • •

The difference between Genius and Talent—Genius is inborn, Talent is developed by hard work.

Intellect and Intelligence—Intellect is ingenerate, Intelligence is the result of experience, guided by enlightened egoism.

Wisdom and Knowledge—Wisdom is knowledge that has not been found wanting, Knowledge when not judiciously used is simply a memory of a fact.

Cleverness and Tact—Cleverness is incipient genius, Tact is talent and egoism profitably blended.

> "Self-love is more artful than the most artful of men."[065]
>
> —La R.

> "Self-love, as it happens to be well or ill-conducted, constitutes virtue and vice. Human prudence rightly understood is circumspect enlightened self-love."[066]
>
> —La R.

> "Self-love is the instrument of preservation; it resembles the provision for the perpetuity of mankind; it is necessary, it is dear to us, it gives us pleasure, and we must conceal it."[067]
>
> —Voltaire.

> "Self-love in a well-regulated breast is as the steward of the household, superintending the expenditure, and seeing that benevolence herself shall be prudential, in order to be permanent, by providing that the reservoir which feeds should also be fed."[068]
>
> —Colton.

---

065   Quoted from "The Wit, Wisdom and Wickedness of La Rochefoucauld" in *The Eagle and The Serpent* Volume 2 Number 1 (September 1900). In turn quoting *Maxims*.
066   *Ibid.*
067   *A Philosophical Dictionary* (1764)
068   Charles Caleb Colton (1780 - 1832). Lapsed clergyman, gambler, author. Coined the phrase "Imitation is the sincerest of flattery." Quote from *Lacon, or Many Things in Few Words, Addressed to Those who Think* (1820).

"It is allowed that the cause of most action, good or bad, may be resolved into love of ourselves; but the self-love of some men inclines them to please others, and the self-love of others is wholly employed in pleasing themselves. This makes the great distinction between vice and virtue, and between the action of the Conscious and Unconscious egos."[069]

—Dean Swift.

"Conceit is the lowest form of self-love; vanity is the highest."

"Love is of all sentiments the most egotistical; therefore, when it is wounded, it is the least generous."[070]

—B. Constant.

"Love unrequited is hatred ignited, because vanity has been slighted."

---

069   Jonathan Swift (1667 - 1745). Author. Original quote from "Thoughts on various subjects" (1726) reads as follows: "The motives of the best actions will not bear too strict an inquiry. It is allowed that the cause of most actions, good or bad, may he resolved into the love of ourselves; but the self-love of some men inclines them to please others, and the self-love of others is wholly employed in pleasing themselves. This makes the great distinction between virtue and vice. Religion is the best motive of all actions, yet religion is allowed to be the highest instance of self-love."

070   Henri-Benjamin Constant de Rebecque *aka* Benjamin Constant (1767 - 1830). Quote from *Adolphe* (1816) " Je voulus réveiller sa générosité, comme si l'amour n'était pas de tous les sentiments le plus égoïste, et, par conséquent, lorsqu'il est blessé, le moins généreux." In turn quoted in *A Case for Wagner* by F. Nietzche (1888).

On Capital and Labor

"It is not capital nor labor that creates wealth and power, but mind."[071]

—Lord Haldane.

Three Forces in the Creation of Wealth or Value

1st *The Psychologist*: Schemer, Planner or Exploiter. He creates by bringing into being something which did not exist, beginning a plan of procedure or a scheme of production—a system of revaluation of values; he moulds matter by the magic of mind. Thus he brings about a new method of production, distribution, exchange and consumption.

2nd *The Worker*: He produces but does not create. He works according to directions from his superiors—the psychic exploiters. As a producer, he builds of already existing things; he is the servant of directive ability—a hireling with limited knowledge of production. He can do well the turning of a handle, or similar piece meal work. He is a cog in the wheel of production, or a nut in the hub of development, but is not so valuable as machinery. He is a segment of science, humanized, specialized, sectionalized and organized by others to his and their own advantage.

3rd *The Consumer*: He makes wealth, because he uses the product and creates the demand for more to replace that which is already consumed. Without consumption, production must stop, because neither the exploiter nor the worker can live or thrive, deprived of the value made possible by the consumer.

The consumer is the real regulator of values—use value, exchange value, or intrinsic value. Therefore, the Directive Mind moulds and makes the destiny of labor—unconscious of its own power.

---

071   Richard Burdon Haldane (1856 - 1928). Lord Chancellor. Original quote from *The Future of Democracy* (1918): "What creates wealth is knowledge and power of diredling the requisite Labour and Capital."

Surplus Value

The products of the remainder of his labor are what Marx called "Surplus Value,"[072] meaning by this phrase all the output of wealth which is beyond what is practically necessary to keep the laborer alive.

The Surplus Value goes to the capitalist, and rightly so, for he creates it. Without his method of production such value would not be.

• • •

If Capitalism is to be blamed for the evils of today, it also must be credited with the blessings that have come to humanity since it began, 150 years ago.

• • •

The successful Capitalist is a credit to his creditors and a benefactor his debtors. He is also a blessing to the workers, for he finds work for them at his own expense, and profits from their own experience and energy.

Not till the capitalists came upon the scene did the workers wear a white collar. A boiled white shirt was unknown among the workers before capitalism controlled production.

The more capitalists there are in a country, the more prosperous is that country. The workers are better off and live on a plane of comfort unknown in non-capitalistic USA. They have today more luxuries than did kings and emperors 100 years ago.

• • •

Workers' Savings

There are $22,000,000,000 in the banks of the US belonging to the workers. This represents the surplus value of their labors, over and above the cost of living. The theory that the worker gets only enough to enable him to live and produce his kind must be abandoned in fact of this mighty fact.

072   Karl Marx (1818 - 1883). Philosopher. Author of *Theories of Surplus-Value* (c1863), co-author of *The Communist Manifesto* (1848).

This amount of money is sufficient to buy out most all of the big capitalists in the country, if they would sell out. The workers would then have the tools of production in their own hands but these tools are not enough to enable the workers to be successful. The tool of thought is the one thing needed in production, and this the workers do not possess in any marked degree.

If the workers were wise and wanted all they say they produce, they might hire the capitalists to show them how to manage successfully, instead of being employed, they could employ their former employers and thus exploit their former exploiters.

The surplus value of the wealth thus created would be their own. The next question is: Could the workers keep it after they had gotten it? It takes a cool head to keep wealth without waste and survive with success.

On the other hand, if the workers create all wealth, or produce all value, why don't they prepare their own plan of production, own their own machinery and do business on their own and in opposition to the capitalists? The answer is: they don't know how. Production on successful lines requires personality. Personality with a purpose, a plan, a program, supported by psychic sagacity, mental audacity and dynamic capacity.

• • •

The measure of success is the measure of desire, engineered by Will. The worker can never be rescued from pain, privation and paralogy, nor can salvation from starvation, superstition and slavery be found until a new plan of production is built on equal consciousness and an omniparity of interests.

Psychology determines the economics of the rich; economics determines the life of the poor.

Directive labor creates wealth. Directed labor increases the value of directive ability and perpetuates wealth. Land, labor and capital was the old slogan, that that all wealth came from this source. The new formula is: Psychic sagacity (or directive ability), capital, machinery, and labor. These are the four forces of production. Labor is the fourth element in production and the least important because it can always be replaced.

If directive ability is taken away from the process of production the result is failure and profitlessness. Capital and labor are not sufficient to produce wealth; this is proven by the thousands of bankruptcies last year. The missing link in success was directive ability.

Labor is the pageboy of progress and the most favored part in the scheme of production. It is paid for whether the scheme is successful or not and is paid before profits are made. Labor costs more than 50 percent or more of the costs of production, and assumes no responsibility for losses in the cost of production.

• • •

The iron law of inequality[073] must be understood before the iron law of wages holds good. Not by economic necessity must salvation be sought, but by equal consciousness on the same plane of consciousness must men seek salvation.

• • •

If the people were to withdraw their savings, they could buy out the steel trust, the shipbuilding industry, the cotton industry, the lumber, wool, rubber and meat-packing businesses. The people of New York alone had $7,914,000,000 in savings accounts up to June 30, 1924.

• • •

Capitalism is the march of man from the complexity of simplicity to the simplicity of complexity.

How simple is the complex printing press to the worker, and how complex to the onlooker.

The laborer is worthy of his hire—and his ire.

Capitalism is the conquest of man over the mass-mind.

Civilization is the conquest of man over matter, materials, machinery and drudgery.

---

073   The phrase "iron law of inequality" was chapter two of Lothrop Stoddard's *The Revolt Against Civilization: The Menace of the Under Man* (1922), though we're unsure if there is any direct link between usages. Of interest, it was later used in Murray N. Rothbard's *Egalitarianism as a Revolt Against Nature, and Other Essays*.

•••

The Working Class

The more perfectly organized the working class is, the more the workers become a class and the more useful and manageable they are; thus the chance of emancipation from their thraldom is more remote. In fact, the gulf is ever and ever widening, and therefore they can never clash with capital.

> Two objects preceding in different directions can never meet. Mankind is segregating and segregation is a factor in evolution. A higher form is in the process of production. Evolution goes on apace beyond man.
>
> —Nietzsche.

A Few Laws of Nature, Considered in These Pages

Spencer's Law of the Survival of the Fittest.[074]

Darwin's Law of Variation of Species.[075]

Newton's Law of Gravity.[076]

Mendell's Law of Heredity.[077]

LaPlace's Law of Acquired Characteristics.[078]

Weismann's Law.[079]

The Law of the Adaptability to Environment.

The Law of the Conservation of Energy.

The Law of Logic.

The Law of Reason.

The Law of Vibration.

The Law of Affinity.

The Law of Polarity.

The Law of Compensation.

The Law of Reciprocity.

074 Herbert Spencer (1820 - 1903). Biologist. Coined the phrase "survival of the fittest" in *Principles of Biology* (1864).
075 Charles Darwin (1809 - 1882). Biologist. Author of *On the Origin of Species* (1859).
076 Isaac Newton (1642 - 1727). Physicist. Author of *Philosophiae Naturalis Principia Mathematica* (1687).
077 Gregor Johann Mendel (1822 - 1884). Biologist. Founder of genetics.
078 Pierre-Simon, marquis de Laplace (1749 - 1827). Mathematician. Discovered double exponential distribution.
079 Friedrich Leopold August Weismann (1834 - 1914). Biologist. Discovered germ plasm theory.

The Law of Attraction.

The Law of Abundance.

The Law of Friendship.

The Law of Sympathy.

The Law of Sensation.

The Iron Law of Wages.

Adam Smith's Law: Labor creates all wealth.[080]

Lord Haldane's Law: Mind makes wealth.[081]

Karl Marx's Law of Economic Determinism.

Like attracts like, etc., etc., etc.

Competition is the law of development.

Co-operation is the first law of weakness.

Co-operation is the law of increasing returns.

Belief in others is the law of democracy.

Belief in self is the law of the successful.

Change is the law of Evolution.

Evolution is retail revolution; revolution is wholesale evolution. The first is rapid revolution; the second is rapid evolution.

Sympathy is the law of congeniality and solace of soul.

Affection is the law of affinity.

Sympathy is the serene part of selfishness.

The line of least resistance is the law of the unfit and other unfinished units of humanity. The line of most resistance is the law of the pilgrim of progress.

The law of progressive life is strife.

The law of progress is exploitation.

The law of love is propagation.

The law of life is Egoism.

The law of Egoism is Selfishness.

---

080   Adam Smith (1723 - 1790). Economist. Author of *An Inquiry into the Nature and Causes of the Wealth of Nations* (1776).
081   Richard Burdon Haldane (1856 - 1928). Lord Chancellor.

Thought-Throbs

The New Golden Rule

Do unto yourself that which you would like others to do unto you, and do unto others that which they would do unto themselves. Then everybody would be satisfied.

The rule of reason says: Rule yourself.

The pleasure that gives no pain is to be embraced.

The pain that gives no pleasure is to be avoided.

The pleasure that prevents a greater pleasure and produces pain is to be avoided.

The pain that prevents a greater pain and secures pleasure is to be accepted.

If the Reform-maniac spent as much time on self culture as he does on trying to convince others that he has a panacea for all the ills of the body politic, he would be valuable as a living example of what could be done with raw material. If the progressive Egoist would begin at home to improve, educate and develop himself, before wasting his time trying to save the world, the world would soon be safe for Aristocracy.

Only the survivors really believe in the survival of the fittest.

Your fate is shaped by your thoughts, your destiny is changed by your actions.

No man is interested in anything that doesn't concern him. That is why it is so easy to bear other people's misfortunes. We are only concerned with our own.

All sorts and conditions of men are searching for panaccas to escape the pangs of impecuniosity and the results of ignorance, apathy, indifference, poverty and misery.

That part of your Ego that knows is to be found above the nose. He who knows he knows is a credit to his nose—and himself.

On Self-love

"Self-love and reason to one end aspire."[082]

—Pope.

"Self-love leads men of narrow minds to measure all mankind by their own capacity."[083]

—Jane Porter.

"Our self-love can he resigned to the sacrifices of everything but itself."[084]

—La Harpe.

"Self-love is not so vile a thing as self-neglecting."[085]

—Shakespeare.

"Of all mankind each loves himself the best."[086]

—Terence.

"All other love is extinguished by self-love; beneficence, humanity, justice, philosophy sink under it."[087]

—Landor.

"It is falling in love with our own mistaken ideas that makes fools and beggars of half mankind."[088]

—Young.

Explore the dark recesses of the mind, in the soul's hunt'st volume read mankind, and own, in wise and simple, great and small, the great same principle in all.

---

082   Alexandar Pope (1688 - 1744). Author. Quote from "An Essay on Man: Epistle II" (1734).

083   Jane Porter (1776 - 1850). Novelist. In the original edition of *Gospel...* this quote was attributed to a "James Porter." It's a popular quote for quote books, though none seem to cite the source.

084   Jean-François de La Harpe (1739 - 1803). Playwright. Another unattributed quote commonly found in quote books.

085   William Shakespeare (c1564 - 1616). Playwright. Quote from *Henry the Fifth* (1599) reads "Self-love, my Liege, is not so vile a sin as self-neglecting."

086   Publius Terentius Afer (195 BC - c159 BC). Playwright.

087   Walter Savage Landor (1775 - 1864). Author. Quote from *Imaginary Conversations* by Landor, attributed to Epicurus in the original edition of *Gospel...*

088   Edward J. Young (1681 - 1765). Theologian. Quote from *A Vindication of Providence, or, A True Estimate of Human Life* (1737).

"For parent and for child, for wife and friend
Our first great move, and our last great end
Is one and by whatever name you call
The ruling Tyrant, Self, is all in all."[089]

—Churchill.

"The best thing a man could know is himself."[090]

"To know thyself—in others self-concern
W'oulds't thou know others? Read thyself and learn."[091]

—Schiller.

"He that knows himself knows others, and he that is ignorant of himself could not write a very profound lecture on other men's heads."

—Colton.

"The world is governed by love-self-love."

"Self-love was born before love."[092]

—De Finod.

"The world is governed by self-interest only."[093]

—Schiller.

"The virtues are lost in self-interest, as rivers in the sea."

—La Rochefoucauld.

"Offended self-love never forgives."[094]

—Étienne Vigée.

"Selfishness if but reasonably tempered with wisdom, is not such an evil trait."[095]

—Ruffini.

---

089   Charles Churchill (1732 - 1764). Satirist. Quote from *The Conference* (1763).
090   "Know Thyself" was inscribed in stone at the Temple of Apollo at Delphi.
091   Johann Christoph Friedrich von Schiller (1759 - 1805). Poet. Quote from *Tabulae Votivae* (1796).
092   J. De Finod, comp., trans. *A Thousand Flashes of French Wit, Wisdom, and Wickedness*. New York: D. Appleton & Co., (1886). Many of these quotes were folded into Bartleby, and may be Seklew's source.
093   Johann Christoph Friedrich von Schiller (1759 - 1805). Poet.
094   Louis-Jean-Baptiste-Étienne Vigée (1758 - 1820). Playwright. Quote misatributed to Nietzche, at it was in the first edition of *Gospel....* Quote from *Les Aveux Difficiles*, scene VII.
095   Giovanni Ruffini (1807 - 1881). Playwright.

"Selfishness is that detestable vice which no one will forgive in others, yet no one is without it. So unreal, that it can never become material, or actual, except by Conscious Egoists on the same plane of Wisdom and Power."[096]

—Lord Kames.

• • •

Human evolution is Egoistic, and individual, before it becomes Social.

• • •

Envy is the homage paid by inferior organisms to their superiors.

• • •

Emulation is the homage, paid by Aspiring Egos, to those whom they desire to resemble.

• • •

Love is a bribe. Nature bribes man to induce him to produce his kind. Pleasure seeking man needs some Compensation before he will undertake to do anything that requires effort. He will not do anything without reward; satisfaction of soul; gratification of the Ego, or some tangible gain.

• • •

Altruism is self-love, expressing itself through a desire to make mankind admire the Altruist.

• • •

Tears from the eyes of an onion are like the tears from the eye of an enlightened Ego—they leave an impression.

• • •

Man is a paradox; a fragment of force; a remnant of yesterday.

• • •

"Ignorance is the mother of fear."[097]

—Lord Kames.

"The common curse of mankind and folly is ignorance."[098]

—Shakespeare.

---

096   Henry Home, Lord Kames (1696 - 1782). Philosopher.
097   Quote from *Sketches of the History of Man, Volume I* (1807) reads "Ignorance is the mother of devotion, to the church and to lawyers."
098   Quote from *Troilus and Cressida* (c1602) reads "The common curse of mankind, folly and ignorance, be thine in great revenue!"

The Gospel According to Malfew Seklew

"Thou monster, ignorance."[099]

—Shakespeare.

"Ignorance never settles a question."[100]

—Beaconsfield.

"They must assume who know the least."[101]

—Gay.

"Ignorance is the dominion of absurdity."[102]

—Froude.

"Who ever is ignorant is vulgar; who ever is vulgar is ignorant."[103]

—Cervantes.

"There is no calamity like ignorance."[104]

—Richter.

"What ignorance there is in human minds."[105]

—Ovid.

"Ignorance is the greatest of all human infirmities."[106]

—Orace Walter.

"It is with narrow-minded people as with narrow-necked bottles; the less they have in them, the more noise they make on pouring it out."[107]

—Pope.

---

099   Quote from *Love's Labor's Lost* (c1590s) reads "O! thou monster Ignorance, how deformed dost thou look!"
100   Benjamin Disraeli, 1st Earl of Beaconsfield (1804 - 1881). Prime Minister. Quote from a speech in House of Commons May 14, 1866. This and some other quotes might have been sourced from *Edge Tools Of Speech* edited by Maturin Murray Ballou 1899.
101   John Gay (1685 - 1732). Poet. Quote from "The Bear in a a Boat" from *Fifty One Fables* (1721) reads: "By ignorance is pride increased / those most assume who know the least."
102   James Anthony Froude (1818 - 1894). Biographer of Thomas Carlyle.
103   Miguel de Cervantes Saavedra (1547 - 1616). Author. *Don Quixote de la Mancha, Book 4* as translated by John Ormsby in *The Complete Works of Miguel de Cervantes Saavedra* (1901): "And do not suppose, senor, that I apply the term vulgar here merely to plebians and the lower orders; for everyone who is ignorant, be he lord or prince, may and should be included among the vulgar."
104   Johann Paul Friedrich Richter aka Jean Paul (1763 - 1825). Author. Quote from *Titan* (1863).
105   Publius Ovidius Naso (43 BC - c18 AD). Poet. Quote from *Fastorum Libri*. Original Latin: "Quantum animis erroria inest!"
106   Izaak Walton (1594 - 1683). Author. Quote source unknown, but expanded quote is as follows: "So long as thou art ignorant, be not ashamed to learn. Ignorance is the greatest of all infirmities; and when justified, the chiefest of all follies."
107   Quote from *Thoughts on Various Subjects* (1727).

"It is with nations as it is with individuals, those who know the least of others, think the highest of themselves."[108]

—Colton.

"It is thus we walk through the world like the blind not knowing whither we are going, regarding as bad what is good, and regarding as good what is bad, and ever in entire ignorance."[109]

—Madam de Servigse.

"Do not take the yardstick of your ignorance to measure what the ancients knew, and call everything which you do not know—lies."[110]

—Phillips.

"Without knowledge there can be no sure progress. Vice and barbarism are the inseparable companions of ignorance."[111]

—Charles Summer.

• • •

Cultivate the social instinct, and give away your kindest thoughts. Cultivate the art of giving, for it is more blessed to give than to receive. Give till you like to give away the surplus value of your Ego. Give until you become a Supercrat.

• • •

The greatest Civilizer is Enlightened Selfishness as expressed through the Socialization of Selfishness and the Cultivation of the Social Instinct to a point when the Ego finds pleasure in distributing the surplus value of his own Ego and giving it away with sympathy and serenity.

The greatest and most beneficent form of Co-operation is that brought about by the grouping of Congenial Souls on

---

108   Charles Caleb Colton. Quote from *Lacon* reads: "It is with nations as with individuals, those who know the least of others, think the highest of themselves; for the whole family of pride and ignorance are incestuous, and mutually beget each other."
109   Marie de Rabutin-Chantal, marquise de Sévigné (1626 - 1696). Aristocrat. Quote from *Letters*.
110   Wendell Phillips (1881 - 1884). Abolitionist.
111   Charles Summer (1811 - 1874). Politician. Quote from *The Works of Charles Sumner* (1870).

the same plane of Consciousness or Self-Understanding. Equal Consciousness is necessary before harmony, peace and concord is possible among men and before sympathy can be scientifically and discreetly distributed to the satisfaction of all in the Group.

Human Nature never changes. It is only our tastes and our opinions that change, as we change our minds.

> "Harmonious society can be created on no other ground than the strictest individuality of interests and responsibilities; nor can the liberty of mankind be restored upon any other principle or mode of action."[112]
>
> —Josiah Warren.

Prejudice which sees what it pleases cannot see what is plain.

Organization: The ability to shift work onto others which produces the most efficient results.

Laughter is a gurgle from the golden lute of life.

Laughter will stab a sneer, soothe a tear; crown a cheer.

Passion subsides where laughter presides (resides).

> "Nothing," says Goethe, "is more significant of men's character than where they find laughter."[113]

A laugh begins with a gurgle of glee, which is joy in a minor key; it then extends to a smite of self-satisfaction, and ends as an eruption of ecstacy—in the form of a laugh.

• • •

First change your mind, then your tastes will change; then alter your methods, then your ways, your habits, and then you can change your environment to suit your own desires.

• • •

---

112 Josiah Warren (1798 - 1874). Individualist anarchist. First anarchist in the United States. Quote from *Equitable Commerce* (1852): "Harmonious society can be erected on no other ground than the strictest individuality of interests and responsibilities; nor can the liberty of mankind be restored upon any other principle or mode of action."

113 Johann Wolfgang von Goethe (1749 - 1832). Author. Quote from *The Maxims and Reflections of Goethe* (1906).

Politics begin with promises and end with compromise.

The voice of the real god is heard when selfishness is understood.

Opportunity: Man today is standing on the threshold of thought, gazing into space, looking for an opportunity to increase power.

Idleness is the mother of invention, and the father of easy times—when the invention is profitable.

Mutual aid is mutually made.

When an honest man sees the truth of a thing, he will not be afraid to say so, when it is considered commendable to speak the truth, without blushing, for fear of Mrs. Grundy and Mr. Pecksniff.[114]

Manners consist in flattering the pride of others and concealing our own. The first step is to conceal our good opinion of ourselves. The next is more impudent, namely, to pretend that we value others more than ourselves. The Moralist practices this method and denounces it at the same time.

"The more it changes, the more it remains the same."
—French proverb.

"Unanimity is the only Compatibility; we are all Egoists."
—R. G.

"History cannot repeat itself, because the individual is unique."
—R. G.

"The most selfish thing I know is generosity; but what a Selfishness!"[115]
—Greville.

"The amount of intellect necessary to please us, is a most accurate measure of the amount of intellect we have ourselves."[116]
—Helvetius.

---

114   "Mrs. Grundy" is a name associated with busybodies and scolds. "Mr. Pecksniff" is a hypocritical character from *Martin Chuzzlewit* (1843) by Charles Dickens (1812 - 1870).

115   Charles Cavendish Fulke Greville (1794 - 1865). Diarist. Quote from *Maxims* (1756) reads "The most selfish thing I know in the world is generosity; but what a Selfishness!"

116   Claude-Adrien Helvetius (1715 - 1771). Philosopher. Quote from *De L'homme* (c1818).

"There is no man alone, because every man is a microcosm and carries the whole world about him."[117]

> —Browne in *Religio-Medici*.

"The more a man has in himself, the less he will want from other people, the less, indeed, other people can be to him. That is why a high degree of intellect tends to make a man unsocial."[118]

> —Schopenhauer in *Wisdom of Life*.

"The road to ambition is too narrow for friendship; too crooked for love; too rugged for honesty, and too dark for science."[119]

> —Rousseau.

"Insist on yourself—never imitate."[120]

> —Emerson.

"The more we study, the more we discover our ignorance."[121]

> —Shelley.

"There are three things too wonderful for me, nay, four things I do not understand: an eagle in the air, a serpent on a rock, a ship in the center of the sea, and a man with a mind."[122]

"All who enjoy work win success, and must share it, for happiness was born a twin." [123]

---

117   Sir Thomas Browne (1605 - 1682). Author. Quote from *Religio Medici* (1643).
118   Quote from *The Wisdom of Life* (1809).
119   Jean-Jacques Rousseau (1712 - 1778). Philosopher. We could find this quote attributed to Rousseau in a number of American newspapers, but not in an original source.
120   Ralph Waldo Emerson (1803 - 1882). Author. Quote from *Essays: First Series* (1841).
121   Percy Bysshe Shelley (1792 - 1822). Poet. Quote from Scenes from the *Magico Prodigioso* (1822).
122   Proverbs 30:18-19 (King James Version) reads: "There be three things which are too wonderful for me, yea, four which I know not: The way of an eagle in the air; the way of a serpent upon a rock; the way of a ship in the midst of the sea; and the way of a man with a maid."
There is a closer translation in Matthew Henry's (1662-1714) commentary on the Bible, but the key difference is they all end with the word "maid," rather than "mind." It was probably intentionally altered, as other quotes in *Gospel...* have been.
123   George Gordon Noel, 6th Baron Byron (1788 1824). Poet. Quote from *Don Juan* (1819).

and Other Writings By and About Sirfessor Wilkesbarre   **127**

"Life is mostly froth and bubble,
Two things stand as stone;
Kindness in another's troubles,
Courage in your own."[124]

—Lindsay Gordan, Australian poet.

"Only 3 to 5 per cent of the human family, as yet, have required the art of thinking; the rest betray their simian-like ancestry by imitation."[125]

—Prof. Huxley.

"True genius is the ray that flings
A flood of light o'er common things."[126]

Every great institution is but the lengthened shadow of some great man.[127]

There are a thousand opportunities today, to one a hundred years ago.

• • •

"Lord of a thousand worlds am I, and I've reigned since time began; and night and day in cyclic sway, shall pass while their deeds I can. Yet time shall cease ere I find release—for I am the Soul of Man."[128]

• • •

Oh, learn to love yourself;
Consider how the silent sun is rapt
In self-devotion! All things work for good
To them that love themselves.

---

124   Adam Lindsay Gordon (1833 - 1870). Poet. Quote from *Sea Spray and Smoke Drift* (1867) reads: " Life is mostly froth and bubble / Two things stand like stone / Kindness in another's trouble / Courage in your own."
125   Thomas Henry Huxley PC FRS FLS (1825 - 1895). Biologist. Though we couldn't find the quote above, this one did catch our attention enough to include it:"I do not hesitate to express my opinion that, if there is no hope of a large improvement of the condition of the greater part of the human family: if it is true that the increase of knowledge, the winning of greater dominion over Nature which is its consequence, and the wealth which follows upon that domination, are to make no difference in the extent and the intensity of Want, with its concomitant physical and moral degradation, among the masses of the people, I should hail the advent of some kindly comet, which would sweep the whole affair away, as a desirable consummation." *Government: Anarchy or Regimentation* (1890).
126   George Brimley (1819 - 1857) attributes this maxim to "the author of "Modern Antiquities" in his 1858 book *Essays*.
127   Slight variation attributed to Ralph Waldo Emerson, but no source.
128   Quote by Charles H. Orr, appearing in *The Theosophical Forum* Volume 4 Number 1 (May 1899).

Urban: "He has another use for mishaps Than to regret them."
Pasqual: "What may that be?"
Urban: "Why, To digest them, Pasqual. Hence have we brains. A mental mastication, slow and sure,
Eupeptic consciences and willful blood
Transform our blunders to experience, sinew
And staple of all wisdom.

Learn to forgive yourself;
Though you were Judas, learn to forgive yourself.
You grant humanity consists of men?
I am a man; so when I serve myself
I serve humanity.[129]

—John Davidson.

Nature is honest with those who are honest with her. As physical exercise strengthens and upbuilds the body, so does psychic exercise elevate and en-noble the Ego.

An over sensitive Conscience is simply the evidence of spiritual dyspepsia. The man who has it is no better than his fellows.

A revelation is worth more than a revolution to an enlightened evolutionist, because it brings one nearer to a realization of one's resolutions.

Association gives warmth; co-operation brings strength; socialization brings happiness; realization brings peace and power.

Without a vision there is no progress

Clodhoppers may improve the landscape, but they seldom improve their minds.

A man's forehead is the frontispiece of his own future and the headstone of his own fate.

"Nature cannot get from winter to summer without a spring, nor from summer to winter without a fall."

Conscious Man is no puppet of Fate, or Chance. He is the Director of his own Destiny, and the incarnation of infinite

129   John Davidson (1857 - 1909). Poet. Paraphrased from "Self's the Man" (1901). Also appears in *The Eagle and The Serpent* Number 18,

power. He can overthrow all obstacles that stand in his way because he knows how to regulate the pulse of his own personality and direct the action of his own mentoids.

The remedy for the removal of most of the evils of today is to learn how to socialize your selfishness, develop your social instinct, increase the circumference of your consciousness, develop a true sense of proportion, acquire the art of compromise, the outcome of which will be a real spirit of justice and equity, expressed in amity and Supercratic sanity. By giving away the surplus value of the Ego to congenial souls tinctured by thought and reinforced by reason will make for harmony and happiness among mankind.

The Supercrat can analyze avarice, ambition, anguish, anger and agony—without tears, or self torture.

Social Aristocracy will produce more equality among men than the Socialist who demands equal opportunity for all, because the Social Aristocrat will consciously strive for betterment and get results, while the Socialists will yearn for results and get disappointment—and perhaps disillusionment.

• • •

"Thinking makes the man."[130]

—Alcott.

"Thought is the seed of action."[131]

—Emerson.

"Thinkers are scarce as gold."[132]

—Lavater.

"Thinking, not growth, makes manhood."[133]

—Isaac Taylor.

---

130 Amos Bronson Alcott (1799 - 1888). Philosopher. Quote appears in *Ford News* Volume 3 Number 3 (1 December 1922).
131 Ralph Waldo Emerson (1803 - 1882). Author. Quote from "Thought on Art" in *The Dial* Volume 1 Number 3 (1 January 1841).
132 Johann Kaspar Lavater (1741 - 1801). Poet. Quote appears in *Ford News* Volume 3 Number 3 (1 December 1922).
133 Isaac Taylor (1759 - 1829). Author. Quote from "Advice to the Teens" (1818). Quote also appears in *Ford News* Volume 3 Number 3 (1 December 1922).

"Learning without thought is labor lost."[134]

—Confucius.

"Man by thinking only, becomes truly man."[135]

—Pestalozzi.

"Nothing is so practical as thought."[136]

—Cecil.

"As a man thinketh in his heart, so is he."[137]

—Proverbs.

"There is no thought in any mind but it quickly tends to convert itself into a power."[138]

—Emerson.

"Youth at the helm, and impulse at the prow;
That is the way to boss creation now.
He only, among publicists is sound,
Who keeps his ear glued closely to the ground."[139]

"Philanthropy moves slaves to tears."

"Justice never pats anyone on the back."

"Never beg what is your own."

"The mistakes of the brave are worth more than the successes of cowards."

War, play, laughter, profanity, alcohol—all conduce to man's relaxation, to his relief from the daily psychic pressure of worry, anxiety, and economic strife. Not much new in all this, you may

---

134   Confucius (551BC - 479BC). Founder, Confucianism. Quote also appears in *Ford News* Volume 3 Number 3 (1 December 1922).

135   Johann Heinrich Pestalozzi (1746 - 1827). Educator. Quote appears in *Ford News* Volume 3 Number 3 (1 December 1922).

136   Quote also appears in *Ford News* Volume 3 Number 3 (1 December 1922).

137   Proverbs 23:7 reads "For as he thinketh in his heart, so is he: Eat and drink, saith he to thee; but his heart is not with thee." Quote also appears in *Ford News* Volume 3 Number 3 (1 December 1922).

138   Ralph Waldo Emerson (1803 - 1882). Author. Quote from "Representative Men" (1850). Quote also appears in *Ford News* Volume 3 Number 3 (1 December 1922).

139   Quote from "The Napoleonic Maxims" appearing in *Change for a Halfpenny: Being the Prospectus of the Napolio Syndicate* (1905).

and Other Writings By and About Sirfessor Wilkesbarre

say. Very well, but worth being called to your attention now and then.

> "Ye who listen with credulity to the whisper of fancy, and peruse with eagerness the phantom of hope, who expect that age will perform the promises of youth, and the the deficiencies of the present day will be supplied by the morrow, must be disappointed as experience is accumulated and wisdom grows."[140]
>
> —Dr. S. Johnson.

Man is the maker of things material; woman is the creator of things psychical. During the period of gestation she moulds the Ego to be, to her psychic desires, and leaves her impingements upon it in the shape of a poet, an artist, or any kind of a genius.

A Neo-Psychologist is one who dissects the dynamics of the present whilst regulating the destinies of democracy and preparing the present to fit the future.

• • •

Life is more than a breath.
When of breath bereft,
There is nothing left but—Death.

• • •

When you are young you can earn a living; later you make a living; when you are old you get a living—anyhow.

Public opinion is merely the private opinion of some prominent individual expressed in public.

The People. A mystery without a history and not to be found in History.

The People. A metaphysical entity but a physical nonentity.

Envy, malice, jealousy and meanness are the fretful conditions of cheap organisms suffering from ulcerated understandings.

Democracy is the madness of the many for the benefit of the few.

---

140   Samuel Johnson (1709 - 1784). Author. Quote from *The History of Rasselas, Prince of Abissinia* (1759).

Man is the swiftest thing that ever dashed into space—looking for work. He found it, and has been in trouble ever since.

Accord, concord, and Mr. Ford are the three best things in successful production.

> Life is a mystery;
> Man is life's history;
> Death is his destiny;
> Deny it who can. This plot of a plan
> Which unfolds in Man
> Stay where you are
> And tell me the purpose
> Of life—if you can.

• • •

Thought Proverbs

Where there's a thought there's a way.

Beauty is only thought deep.

A rolling thought gathers no moss.

A thought in time saves nine.

A little thinking is a dangerous thing.

It's a long thought that has no turning.

One good thought deserves another.

Handsome is as handsome thinks.

Don't cross a thought until you come to it.

A thought can rise no higher than its source.

Cast your thoughts upon the waters and they will come back after many days.

Never too late to think.

> "In men this blunder still you find,
>   All think their little set mankind."[141]

> —Hannah More.

---

141   Hannah More (1745 - 1833). Poet. Quote from "Florio" (1786).

"Men are never so likely to settle a question rightly as when they discuss it freely."[142]

—Macauley.

"Men are most apt to believe what they least understand."[143]

"A little folly is desirable in him that will not be guilty of stupidity."[144]

"We seek and offer ourselves to be gulled. I have never seen a greater monster or miracle in the world than myself."[145]

—Montague (Montaigne).

"Above all things, reverence yourself."[146]

—Pythagoras.

"None deserve the character of being good who have not spirit enough to be bad; goodness for the most part is either indolence or impotence."[147]

—La Rouchfaucauld.

"Out of fallacies come truth. All great truths originate from falsehood. All great theories are the result of false impressions."[148]

—E. Renan.

Try we lifelong, we can never
Straighten out life's tangled skein,
Why should we, in vain endeavor,
Guess and guess and guess again?
Life's a pudding full of plums;
Care's a cancer that benumbs.
Wherefore waste our elocution
On impossible solution?
Life's a pleasant institution,
Let us take it as it comes. [149]

142   Thomas Babington (or Babbington) Macaulay, 1st Baron Macaulay (1800 - 1859). Poet. Quote from "Southey's Colloquies on Society" (1830).
143   Michel de Montaigne (1533 - 1592). Author. Quote from *Essais, Book III* (1595).
144   *Ibid.*
145   *Ibid.*
146   Pythagoras (c570 BC - c495 BC). Philosopher. Quote from *The Golden Verses of Pythagoras*.
147   Quote from *Reflections; or Sentences and Moral Maxims* (1678). Quote also appears in *The Eagle and The Serpent* Volume 2 Number 1 (September 1900).
148   Joseph Ernest Renan (1823 - 1892). Philosopher.
149   Quote from *The Gondoliers; or, The King of Barataria* (1889) by W. S. Gilbert (1836 - 1911)

The Gospel According to Malfew Seklew

• • •

"A man, however well behaved, At best, is only a monkey—shaved!"[150]

Where is Utopia?

Tell me where;

Straight down that crooked street,

And right round the Square.

If you do not find it there, you'll find it as a vagrant thought underneath your hair.

The Thumb is the Finger of Fate pointing towards selfishness, love and hate, the trinity of power that regulates all forces that propagate, agitate, mediate and operate.

Laughter oils the wheels of wisdom, and lubricates the limbs of Love.

Laughter keeps your face merry and bright, your brain brilliant, and your body all right.

An Epigrin, the latest way a grin to win.

Improved arithmetic: Multiply the virtues of your friends, subtract from their faults, add to their kindnesses, divide their difficulties, practice their excellencies, proportionate their sorrow, and ignore their vulgar fractions.

While the poor pray the profiteers prey upon them.

One ought to profit by the mistakes of the past in order to make a profit out of the present.

Prejudice which sees what it pleases can not see what is plain.

The average man seldom knows all that other men think he knows, but the chances are he knows a few things he isn't suspected of knowing.

• • •

You leave the past behind you as you push past the present; at the same time you take it with you in your mind.

The past is passed, the present is plus the past, and the past and the present makes the future.

---

and Arthur Sullivan (1842 - 1900).

150   Quote from *The Mikado; or, The Town of Titipu* (1885) by W. S. Gilbert and Arthur Sullivan.

I lived in the past. I live in the present. I live for the future. What is the past? Something gone before, leaving behind something which has only just begun—the present. Some people dash into the future regardless of reason; others stay in the present as a protest against the future and as an apology for the past. I push past the past into the future while making a pastime of the present.

• • •

A mind that is too feeble to invent doctrines itself always adopts doctrines invented by others. Consequently we all of us hold a large variety of doctrines regarding a large variety of subjects. We value them partly as helping us to live well, partly as in a measure gratifying our desire for knowledge of the world, but mainly as creeds that we are bound to make prevail. To make them prevail we resort to every conceivable means: rational and irrational, savage and civilized, brutal and humane, force, fear, flattery, bribery, threats, ostracism, prayer, preaching and teaching. Yet most of the doctrines which we thus hold as sacred creeds and solemnly urge upon the world are unintelligible, vague, incoherent, ignorant, shallow, silly—logically rotten.

The remedy? The remedy is criticism—of self.[151]

—Cassius J. Keyser.

"Ultimate psychic processes show that the unconscious is the theatre of the most important mental phenomena."[152]

—Frank.

"Look well into thyself; there is a source which will always spring up if thou wilt always search there."[153]

—Marcus Aurelius.

"Nature and wisdom always vote the same ticket."[154]

151   Cassius J. Keyser. Mathematician. Quote from *Thinking About Thinking* (c1926) ends with: "The remedy? The remedy is criticism. But what kind? I will try to indicate."
152   Quote from *Psychic Phenomena / Science and Immortality* (1916) by Henry Frank (1859 - 1933). In the first edition this was misattributed to Wilhelm Maximilian Wundt (1832 - 1920). Psychologist.
153   Marcus Aurelius (121 - 180). Emperor and Philosopher. Quote from *Meditations, Book VII*.
154   Anonymous. Appears in the *Le Mars Globe Post* for December 27, 1926.

• • •

"Blamed by those, praised by these, I smile at fools, defy the wicked, and hasten to laugh at all, lest I be compelled to weep."[155]

• • •

Thought is moulded into knowledge and wisdom, but
Knowledge and wisdom, far from being one,
Have oft-times no connection, Knowledge dwells,
In heads replete with thoughts of other men,
Wisdom in minds attentive to their own;
Knowledge is proud that she has learned so much,
Wisdom humble that she knows no more.[156]

—Cowper.

What is Life? I ask of you, what is life? Oh, tell me true, is life a joke, or but a clue, please tell me, what is life, will you?

Is life a place where names are filed, or is it but a story wild, that only fits for some young child?

And then in life what do we get, we sit, we stare, we fret. Why, friends, at any time I'll bet that man has not solved life's problems yet.

• • •

Man

Spark of infinity!
Germ of Divinity!
Fire of Prometheus, shrouded in clay;
Doomed to mortality,
Prey to fatality,
Child of Eternity, worm of a clay;
Mind which can compass the stars with its span;
Creature of Mystery!
Marvelous Man.

---

155   Pierre de Beaumarchais (1732 - 1799). Playwright. Quote from *Le Barbier de Séville* (1773).
156   William Cowper (1731 - 1800). Poet. Quote from "The Task" (1785).

• • •

Arch o'er immensity,
Thronged to intensity,
O'er thee vast myriads of wanderers sweep;
Endless their numbers,
For death never slumbers;
Oh! 'tis a sigh at which angels must weep.
Whence are ye flying, dark atoms of clay? Ask the poor
wandereds and what can they say? When shall this mystery
Shrouding man's history,
Burst like a flash on our wandering gaze?
Cut from it's central Sun,
Can the lost planet run
Back to its orbit in splendor to blaze?
Silence, rash mortal! this sentence indite:
"Shall not the Judge of Creation do right?"

"Good God! How rare men are."[157]

—Napoleon.

"I made my generals out of mud."[158]

—Napoleon.

• • •

"It costs a lot to live these days
More than it did of yore;
But when you stop to think of it,
It's worth a whole lot more."

A supergram is a supergem of thought. An apigrin is an epigram garnished with a grin.

All human life is gradually changing from the simple to the complex; from unconsciousness to Ego Consciousness.

Yesterday is dead—forget it! Tomorrow does not exist—don't worry! Today is here—use it!

---

157   Napoleon Bonaparte (1769 - 1821). Emperor. Quote from *The Table Talk and Opinions of Napoleon Buonaparte* (1870).
158   Quote from *The Corsican* (1910).

"Wit is the wishbone of wisdom, the funnybone of fact,
and the touchstone of truth."[159]

—M. S.

Tears: Diamonds in the eye, dimmed by desire denied.

Tears: Tiny globules of grief, finding relief from the tyrant of thought, unsought.

Dirt, like a cheap organism, is matter in the wrong place.

A man who would go on strike for fun, would go to hell for pleasure.

Direct action generally leads direct to reaction.

Man will not do anything for anybody unless he gets some benefit for whatever he does.

All motives are selfish, but all selfishness is not mortification of motive or mutilation of mood.

Thought will abolish evil, for evil is ignorance and ignorance is the cause of evil.

The conscious Egoist seeks the truth wherever it is to he found. As Marcus Aurelius says: I seek after truth, by which no man ever yet was injured.

All wise men and Social Supererats hate poverty, misery, injustice, tyranny, and slavery, thus justifying hatred as an essential element in human behaviour.

A worker gives away his sympathy before he gives away his donations; but the millionaire gives away his donations, with or without sympathy. They both give away first that which they have the most of and value the least.

A Bolshevik is a brainstormer in a snowstorm, looking for something that is not there.

The successful pugulist of today, gifted with psychic sagacity is the finest expression of human endeavor, because he has an invisible hammer in his hand, and an inspiration in his fist; while

---

159   Malfew Seklew.

the average man wears a watch on his wrist, without any risk.

Pleasures of the palate; pleasures of the pelvic region, and pleasures of memory, are the three avenues of joy which everybody enjoys—at their leisure.

The Supercrat travels along the line of greatest attraction even though he meets with death. The Subterman travels along the line of least resistance—even though he meets with slavery.

Man is not a religious, moral, social, or political animal by Nature, but assumes these virtues for selfish reason; the better to enable him to defeat his enemies, and to compete with his friends.

Selfishness radiamized by reason is the Homocea of happiness and the Panacea for pain and parology.

The best preacher is the heart

The best teacher is time!

The best book is the world,

The best friend is Enlightened Selfishness.

Man is a worshipping animal and the instinctive god of his idolatry is Self.

Man is a Natural self worshipper; until by intelligent self-interest he finds himself out—from within—and becomes a self educator.

Undeveloped human beings must believe in something external, because they have no other means of focusing their powers, of condensing their dynamic unity. The developed individual believes in himself, and the principle of self-belief is the essence of western individualism.

> "Most men are at heart individualistic rebels against law
> and custom; the social instincts are later and weaker than
> the individualistic, and need re-enforcement. Man is not
> good by Nature, but through association, if even in the
> family, sympathy comes, a feeling of kind, and at least of
> kindness. We like what is like us, we pity not only a thing
> we have loved, but also one which we judge similar to

ourselves, out of this comes an imitation of emotions, and finally some degree of conscience. Conscience, however, is not innate, but acquired, and varies with geography."[160]

—Spinoza.

"I wish that men would realize where trite progress comes from. Great thinkers, good men, noble thoughts, high ideals, intellectual achievements, patient scientists, and the undimmed truth—those are the forces that make for true progress; those are the forces which are worth more in a country than all forces of race hatred, of militarism, of aggressive strength, of organized brutality."[161]

• • •

The most enlightened period of Greek civilization was the time when Stirpiculture was the fashionable philosophy and its principles were practiced. In 150 years Greek produced more men of genius than the whole world produced in 2000 years.

"Energy, intellect, and pride—these make the Superman. But they must be harmonized; the passions will become powers only when they are selected and unified by some great purpose, which moulds a chaos of desires into the power of a personality."[162]

—Nietzsche.

"The road to the Superman must be through aristocracy. Democracy—this mania for counting noses—must be eradicated before it is too late."[163]

—Nietzsche.

• • •

I am the impulse of every great discoverer, of every benefactor, of every inventor, of everything. I am that which sets every star in the firmament; I am that which forms man—I am an Idea!

• • •

If you want wisdom, you must toil for it; and if pleasure, you

160   Quote attributed to Baruch Spinoza (1632 - 1677) from Durant's *The Story of Philosophy* (1924).

161   Georg Morris Cohen Brandes (1842 - 1927). Critic. Quote from *The Conservator* (March 1917).

162   Quote attributed to Friedrich Nietzsche from Durant's *The Story of Philosophy* (1924).

163   Quote attributed to Friedrich Nietzsche from Durant's *The Story of Philosophy* (1924).

and Other Writings By and About Sirfessor Wilkesbarre   **141**

must toil for it. This is the law. Pleasure comes through toil, and not by self-indulgence and indolence.

The secret of power, intellectual or physical, is concentration.

Develop pluck. Let the other fellow trust to luck. Anybody can do a thing he feels like doing, but it takes a true man to do a thing when he doesn't feel like doing it.

Affinitize your affections—without affectation.

> "When you know a thing to hold that you know it, and when you do not know a thing, to confess that you do not know it, that is knowledge."
>
> —Confucius.

Poverty midst plenty; luxury midst want; will always prevail, as long as cheap organisms are full of travail.

> "Men who have done the best for the world have the best right to be disappointed with the result of their efforts."[164]
>
> —W. E. Adams.

---

164 William Edwin Adams (1832 - 1906). Journalist. Quote from *Memoirs of a Social Atom* (1903).

"With few exceptions, I despise the present generation, and only in humanity as it will be in the future do I find any consolation."[165]

—J. Mazzini.

"The world reserves its big prizes for one thing, and that is Initiation. Initiation is doing the right thing without being told."[166]

One of the great evidences of self-control is the power to forget others who are looking at you. [167]

Don't rail and fret,
Do not forget
That happiness,
Though hidden,
Is ever near
With open car
And comes
When she is hidden.
We seek in vain
In town and plain
For her to woo
And win us,
Let age and youth
Learn this great truth.
She hides—
But hides within us.

---

165   Mathilde Blind *aka* Mathilde Cohen aka Claude Lake (1841 - 1896). Poet. Quote attributed to Giuseppe Mazzini (1805 - 1872) from "Personal recollections of Mazzini" in *Fortnightly Review* Number 49 (May 1891).
166   Elbert Green Hubbard (1856 - 1915). Philosopher. Quote from *Love, Life and Work* (1906) reads: "The world bestows its big prizes, both in money and honors, for but one thing. And that is Initiative. What is Initiative? I'll tell you: It is doing the right thing without being told."
167   Elbert Hubbard. It is known that Hubbard paid writers for work that he attributed to himself, so we cannot be sure of the true source of a Hubbard quote. Egoist writer Benjamin DeCasseres sued Hubbard over the latter publishing a book under his own name, where the material originally "written for hire" by DeCasseres for a Hubbard magazine constituted about 80% of the total material.

"The public! The public! How many fools does it take to make a public!"[168]

—Chamfort.

"For his successful progress, man has been largely indebted to those qualities which he shares with the ape and the tiger; his exceptional physical organization, his cunning, his sociability, his curiosity, his imitation and his ruthless and ferocious destructiveness, when his anger is aroused by opposition."[169]

—Prof. Huxley.

"Our higher civilization is multiplying from its lower specimens, and our voters are being propagated increasingly from idle, unthrifty and unemployable invalids. Scientific men declare that there are nine sorts of idiots and six sorts of madmen. And the curse is that all these fifteen kinds of idiots and madmen are cheerfully multiplying with impunity."[170]

—William Edwin Adams.

"It was not the eating of the apple of knowledge that hurt Adam and Eve; the injury came from not digesting it."[171]

—Dr. Tilden.

"Nothing is impossible to the man who can will, and then do, this is the only way of success."[172]

—Mirabeau.

"One thing about the wages of sin is that a man doesn't have to go to law to collect them."[173]

"In idle wishes, fools supinely stay;
Be there a will, and wisdom finds a why."[174]

—Crabbe.

---

168   Quoted in *The Eagle and The Serpent* Volume 2 Number 2 (October 1900).
169   Quote from *Evolution and Ethics* (1893).
170   William Edwin Adams (1832 - 1906). Journalist. Quote from *Memoirs of a Social Atom* (1903). Attributed to "Harold White" in the first edition of *The Gospel....*
171   John Henry Tilden (1851 - 1940). Physician/Nutritional Crank.
172   Honoré Gabriel Riqueti, comte de Mirabeau (1749 - 1791). Revolutionary.
173   Anonymous. Quote appears in *Lebanon Daily Herald* (October 17, 1914).
174   George Crabbe (1754 - 1832). Poet. Quote from "The Birth of Flattery" (c1919).

• • •

A psychologist can see clearly through the mists of misunderstanding that surrounds the discussion of religious morals, politics, and social questions. A unified outlook is necessary to seek the truth of a problem. Morals and religions can be vivisected as scientifically as any other human manifestation.

> "Tomorrow I will live," the fool doth say; "today it is too late; the wise lived yesterday."[175]

> "The mintage of wisdom is to know that rest is rust, and that real life is in love, laughter and work."[176]
>
> —E. Hubbard.

The reformaniac yearns to do the impossible without attempting to do the probable.

How can the International be possible, before the National is actual.

Temperament is merely another name for temper in a tempest.

The pioneers of thought are the pacemakers of progress.

The death of desire, developed a desire for death. Suicide is santified by sanity, when reinforced by reason.

Luxury is evidence of the existence of progress, for man increases his wants as he increases his capacity to enjoy.

Progress means the ability to satisfy these new desires with promptitude and proper pride.

A soul surcharged with the sunshine of consciousness wears a smile that is sublime.

People co-operate because they want to accumulate happiness, wisdom, wealth or power.

The greed of gain brings progress with pain.

Enlightened selfishness will be the savior of mankind—in the course of time.

Emulation is the highest form of imitation, which tends to

---

175   Marcus Valerius Martialis aka Martial (40 - c104). Poet. Quote from *Epigrams* (c104).
176   Elbert Green Hubbard. Quote references but is not found in *Love, Life and Work* (1906).

bring forth the highest and best form of conduct and consideration.

The Conscious Egoist analyses the present to improve the future, and uses his wisdom to improve his personality. He recognizes, "that Nature and wisdom are never at strife."[177]

Man has no rights. He possesses only one right—the right to think.

> "Man can not be uplifted. He must be seduced into virtue."[178]
>
> —Don Marquis.

> "The highest and rarest form of contentment is approval of the success of another."[179]
>
> —A. Bierce.

> "He who thinks with difficulty believes with alacrity."[180]
>
> —A. B.

> "Man was won to virtue, not by force, but by flattery."[181]
>
> —Mandeville.

> "Mandeville," says Prof. Bain, "was the first writer to affirm that virtue could exist without self-denial."[182]

Self-sacrifice is self-realization and not self-denial at all.

Old men give good advice to console themselves for being no longer a bad example.

Philosophy it seems is no more than an interpretation of the universe in terms of consciousness.

> Youth at the helm, and impulse at the prow;
> That is the way to boss creation now.[183]

177　Quote attributed to Plutarch (46 - 120). Historian.
178　Quote attributed to Donald Robert Perry Marquis (1878 - 1937). Cartoonist.
179　Ambrose Bierce (1842 - c1914). Author. Quote from *A Cynic Looks at Life* (1912).
180　*Ibid.*
181　Bernard de Mandeville (1670 - 1733). Author. Paraphrased from *The Fable of the Bees* (1714).
182　Alexander Bain (1818 - 1903). Philosopher. Quote from *Moral Science; A Compendium of Ethics* (1869).
183　Change for a Halfpenny: Being a Prospectus of the Napolio Syndicate (1905).

• • •

'Twixt optimist and pessimist the difference is droll;
The optimist see the doughnut, the pessimist the hole.

• • •

Humanity can be divided into three parts: Humanity, Jewmanity and Supermanity.

Humanity represents solidity and stupidity; Jewmanity represents Jewplicity, which is a compound of rapacity, audacity, capacity and sagacity; Supermanity represents the last analysis of humanity, and the arrival of the Superman.

• • •

"Man is the Magic Power that moves and makes;
Man is Mind, and ever more he takes
The Tool of Thought, and shaping what he wills,
Brings forth a thousand joys, destroys a thousand ills;
He thinks in secret, and it comes to pass,
Environment is but his Looking Glass."[184]
"We do in moderation the things we don't like, and in excess the things other people don't like us to do."[185]

—O. Wilde.

Experience is a great teacher, but by the time it hands a man his diploma, he is too old to make much use of his knowledge.
"A nation turned out to type by methods of mass production can do anything but create a civilization."

—*New Age.*

"Just as we grow more found of those to whom we have done a kindness, so we hate violently those whom we have greatly injured."[186]

—LaBruyere.

The highest form of civilization is possible only when men and women have acquired the science of socializing their selfishness

---

184 James Allen (1864 - 1912). Poet. Quote from *As a Man Thinketh* (1902).
185 Oscar Fingal O'Flahertie Wills Wilde (1854 - 1900). Poet. Quote from *A Woman of No Importance* (1893) reads: "Moderation is a fatal thing, Lady Hunstanton. Nothing succeeds like excess."
186 Jean de La Bruyère (1645 - 1696). Philosopher. Quote from the posthumous book *Caractères* (1885).

and know the art of giving away the surplus value of their ego with amity, urbanity, sanity and benignity.

Don't talk too much; a stiff lower jaw is as useful as a stiff upper lip.

"The law of necessity controls the inclinations, the will, and the reason."[187]

—Napoleon.

"The past tendency of the human intellect has been to ignore substantial realities, and waste its energies on empty speculations respecting the cause of phenomena."[188]

—Auguste Comte.

As Herbert Spencer says: "There is a soul of goodness in things evil; and also a soul of truth in things erroneous."[189]

"Although all cry, 'Down Self,' none means his own self in a literal sense."[190]

—Butler.

"Every one wishes for his own advantage rather than that of others."[191]

—Terence.

"The force of selfishness is as inevitable and as calculable as the force of gravitation."[192]

—Hillard.

"Man, know thyself; all wisdom centers there."[193]

—Young.

187 Quote from *Napoleon: In His Own Words* (1916) edited by Jules Bertaut.

188 Isidore Auguste Marie François Xavier Comte (1798 - 1857) aka Auguste Comte. Philosopher. Author of *A General View of Positivism* (1865).

189 Quote from *First Principles* (1862) reads: "We too often forget that not only is there 'a soul of goodness in things evil,' but very generally also, a soul of truth in things erroneous." In turn, this references "There is some soul of goodness in things evil / Would men observingly distil it out" from *Henry V* by William Shakespeare (c1564 - 1616).

190 Samuel Butler (1612 - 1680). Poet. Quote from *Hudibras* (c1674).

191 Publius Terentius Afer (c195 BC - 159 BC). Playwright.

192 George Stillman Hillard (1808- 1879). Lawyer. Quote appears in *Great Thoughts From Master Minds* Volume 2 Number 46 (November 15, 1884). Misattributed to a "Willard" in the first edition of *Gospel*....

193 Edward Young (1681 - 1765). Quote from *The Complaint: or, Night-Thoughts on Life, Death, & Immortality* (1742).

"Interest speaks all sorts of tongues and plays all sorts of parts, even the part of the disinterested."[194]

—La R.

"If you isolate yourself. how will it help humanity? He snapped his fingers, 'always that,' he answered. I reform myself, that is the beginning of reform—self. When I have accomplished that, perhaps I shall return and teach others."

—A. Bierce.

"I am chained to the frozen heights of existence, and Truth is the vulture that is gnawing my Vitals."

—Anonymous.

"Every man speaks well of his heart, but no one dares speak well of his head."

—La R.

Poverty consists in being separated from the good things of life, which are the joys of existence.

"The trouble with clever people is the they talk a good deal less than they would if they weren't so clever."[195]

—Anon.

• • •

What a happy old world this would be if men who didn't know anything would only keep it to themselves.

An ounce of intuition may be better than a pound of tuition, for intuition is an instantaneous recognition of a thing; tuition is a slow process and has to be paid for.

• • •

"False modesty is the last refinement of vanity. It is a lie."[196]

—A writer of two centuries ago.

---

194   Quote from *Reflections; or Sentences and Moral Maxims* (1665).
195   Quote appears in *The Smart Set* Volume 45 Number 1 (January 1915). Edited by H. L. Mencken before his journal *The American Mercury*.
196   Jean de La Bruyère. Quote from the posthumous book "Caractères" (1885).

A reformaniac is: a mild maniac who is desirous of reforming everybody except himself. Monomaniac: a monist on the moan—when not alone.

Socialism may not come in a day—nor in the morning: it may come like a nightmare or a thief in the night.

Instinct, Habit and Will make the trinity of Triumph.

> "Ideas mould the destiny of nations and write their characters on the countenance of man. He who gives the world ideas helps to make its history; and the thoughts that occupy the mind of the individual shape his career."

> "Wealth, power and office are all the produce of ideas."
> —J. P. Angeld.

● ● ●

No one has ever been able to explain why men persist in believing that they can be rich, noble, and happy in some manner other than by the exacting processes of Nature. It is a hope that by some kind of necromancy one may obtain the fruits of drudgery, without the drudgery.

> "What we call Luck is simply Pluck,
> And doing things over and over,
> Courage and will,
> Perseverance and skill
> Are the four leaves of Luck's clover."[197]

● ● ●

Let the howlers howl, and the growlers growl,
And the prowlers prowl, and the mugwumps go it.
  Behind the night
  There is plenty of light,
  And things are all right.
  And I know it.

---

197 Quote attributed to "Selected," appears in *Oregon Teachers Monthly* Volume 20 Number 1 (September 1915), and attributed to "Sunshine Bulletin" in a 1916 issue of *Employes Magazine*, a trade journal for railroad employees.

• • •

The reason some people try to do good is because it's so much easier than being good.

Thrills

There are thrills in the glorious brightness of day,
There are thrills in the shadows of night,
There are thrills in the stars of the great Milky Way,
There are thrills in the moon's silv'ry light.
There are thrills in the wonderful journey through life,
There are thrills in the slumber of death.
There are thrills in both leisure and unending strife,
There are thrills in each life-giving breath.
There are thrills in the flash of a cobra's fangs,
There are thrills in the coo of a dove,
There are thrills in the bitter and deadening pangs
Of a heart that is wounded by love.
There are thrills in the grasp of a baby's hand,
There are thrills in a farewell kiss,
There are thrills in the strong and unbreakable band
That life gives to nuptial bliss.
There are thrills in a smile and a glad "hello,"
There are thrills in a sorrowful sigh,
There are thrills in the dreams of long, long ago
There are thrills in a last "good-by."[198]

—A. W. Dragstedt.

In the days that were earlier,
When man's hair was much curlier;
Why he was dumb, he developed a thumb;
And from that thumb, all things have come.

The thumb developed the brain; then the thumb became the first scholar to the brain. First came the rule of thumb; then the rule of reason—and Supermanity.

---

[198]   *The Hobo: The Sociology of the Homeless Man* by Nels Anderson (1923) is Volume 2 of the Chicago School of Criminology series. Anderson describes Dragstedt as born in Sweden "some forty years ago." Dragstedt served as Secretary of the Hobo College for 1922-1923. As Secretary he organized meetings and assembled speakers. "As a high brow, Dragstedt is a poet of no mean ability."

We all live according to our lights, but we all act according to the state of our liver; that is the reason that pink pills for pale people sell so well.

War has a psychological value; it changes values, and owners of the soil, which changes systems of government.

War is the great educator. It destroys rapidly, and enforces rebuilding quickly. It quickens the thoughts of men; hastens inventions; and ennobles the aspirations of woman.

War is a biological necessity, and a psychological blessing, for the fighting instinct must be fostered and sustained in a world of warring atoms, if a nation is to survive.

War will cease when progress ends; and everybody is satisfied with themselves—whenever that may be.

> All that Is, is truth and good—
> The "evil" is negation—
> So, wisely let thine attitude
> Be one of affirmation.
> Nor yet invite a passive mood
> On "trial" and "suffering" never brood—
> With gladness and elation.
> On myself insist, imbued
> Of tranquil resignation.[199]

—R. D. Stocker.

• • •

---

199 R. D. Stocker. Theosophist.

The Constitution of the Supercrat

Supercrats and Egocrats accept and uphold the following as Natural and desirable principles:

The Supremacy of Wisdom, The Leadership of the Supercrat,

The Authority of Evidence and Logic,

The Grouping of Congenial Atoms,

The Commonwealth of Conscious Egos,

That Psychology precedes all progress, as the dreamer precedes the schemer.

That Philosophy is the first born of Psychology, and the science is the first born of Philosophy and the child of Psychology;

That Psychology discovers and conceives; Philosophy examines and formulates; Science manipulates and demonstrates;

That brotherhood is local and largely vocal;

That selfishness is universal and love is local;

That society is not an organism; if it is anything, it is an orgasm;

That self-sacrifice is a deception, and there is no such thing for all attempts at self-sacrifice are efforts made towards self-realization;

That man is the measure of value; mind the measure of wisdom and personality, the measure of power and greatness;

That Super-Woman is the chemist of Consciousness, the alchemist of supermanity, love, life and laughter, the miracle of mentality and the Queen of mirth;

That Super-man is the architect of his own fate and environment;

That all human beings are Egoists—some conscious and

some unconscious;

That all cheap organisms travel along the line of least resistance, in search for happiness, but find instead mostly misery; while Supercrats travel along the lines of most resistance and greatest attraction and find new sensations, wisdom and power;

That surplus value of wealth is not produced by Labor but by psychic sagacity, mental audacity, perspicacious pugnacity and dynamic capacity of the Supercrat;

That resource, energy and enterprise are necessary to success, for without aim, action and ambition nothing is possible, the incentive to victory and personal gain being increased in personal power;

That a militant minority shall always have authority over the majority;

That altruism is a fallacy and churchianity a failure;

That there is no sin but ignorance;

That evolution is slow revolution; revolution is rapid evolution;

That the few initiate and the many imitate;

That Capitalism is a blessing for it affords workers to wear white collars and gold teeth;

That Economic salvation is possible when demanded by Egos on the same plane of Consciousness.

That to get ahead, you must have a head.

• • •

The Gospel According to Malfew Seklew is without dogmas or duty, and is tolerant to all other adherents of all faiths—or none.

It is the gospel for independent minds struggling to be free from fear, doubt, or superstition. It proclaims that man is the atom of progress, and the measure of value, and its object is to glorify Man—the Ego Conscious Organism. It affirms that each creature is capable of reason, and that he is responsible for his own actions—because he is conscious of his possibilities; the creator of circumstances and not the slave of his environment, as are unconscious Egos.

It affirms that Nature is selfish and that Selfishness is God, and that all is good, when properly understood.

That Man is immortal—through Consciousness—and is limited only by the glory of his genius, and the splendor of his imagination and inspirations.

That Conscious Man is a spark of Omnipotence; and a particle of Cosmic Consciousness. That Man alone is responsible for what he is, and what he will be. Being conscious of his powers, he is his own judge and dispenser of his own rewards and punishments. His aim in life is to avoid pain and pursue the pleasures of the palate and the pleasures of the pelvic region—with moderation.

By obeying the 600 laws of Nature, he acquires peace, plenty, pleasure, and power; by destroying the 6,000 illusions, delusions and confused conclusions that beset all mankind, he acquires health, wealth, hope and happiness.

This evangel of enlightenment will, if understood properly, inaugurate a revolution in thought, in morals, in action. and in the art of living. It would force upon the people new desires which would produce new systems, concerning which the people have never been consulted, it would change ancient oppositions by showing how easy it is for Ego Conscious organisms to produce progress and power, garnished with happiness and health. Wisdom will abound, wealth will be plentiful, ignorance will be annihilated, superstition will be strangled to death, and laughter will be lord, where the Supercrats live.

The Gospel According to Malfew Seklew will increase the consciousness of the Ego, enhance his value, improve his outlook, develop his possibilities, intensify his individuality and improve his power of personality.

WHAT IS THE REMEDY?

To eliminate misery, poverty, ignorance and sin from mankind the first thing is to learn how to socialize one's own Selfishness.

Salvation by Selfishness is the only way to peace, plenty and power. Salvation according to economic necessity is impossible, because of the difference in the mentality of those who desire economic security.

Equal consciousness is the one thing needful, before success is possible in any scheme of production or redemption.

All who associate with hope of success must do the right thing, in the right way, at the right time, with no dissenting voice, or discord, instead of concord will prevail.

The Social Instinct must be developed by doing acts of kindness, repeatedly, until one finds great pleasure in so doing.

Distribute the Surplus Value of your Ego, with consideration and discretion. The more you give, the ignore you receive from Society. The joy of giving is intensified by the pleasure of producing; added to which is the bliss of beholding the happiness of the receiver.

Increase the circumference of your consciousness by studying the Laws of Nature. All of which when obeyed bring health, wealth, wisdom and personal power.

Strive to rid the world of those twin enemies of mankind, ignorance and mean selfishness. Ignorance can be abolished by education; but selfishness in all its ramifications can never be extirpated, but may be scientifically handled by the Conscious Egoist, for his own good and for the benefit of mankind.

Learn the difference between ignoble selfishness and noble selfullness. Selfullness is selfishness radiumized by reason, illumined by enlightened self-interest.

Develop a true sense of proportion.

Cultivate a real sense of comparison.

Acquire the art of compromise, because justice is founded

on these three qualities of mind and consciousness. With these forces in operation a real civilization is possible.

> "Behind me is Infinite Power,
> Before me is endless possibility,
> Around me is boundless opportunity." [200]

• • •

A MILLENIUM TO ORDER– WITHOUT DISORDER

Group according to equal consciousness. Purchase land and cultivate it on intensive culture principles, guided by experts, till proficiency is acquired by the groupists. All members of the colony must belong to the Society of Social Supercrats.

Each member to have so much land in his own right, in order to make him economically independent of the group and also to enable him to get the full return of his labor. Enlightened self-interest demands that each Ego must find his own Economic Salvation, either by individual effort, or in co-operation with others.

Industries will be started as necessity demands. Co-operation will be cultivated when it pays better than does individual effort.

Harmony and success is assured, because each member— with equal consciousness—will know when to do the right thing at the right time, for every action will be guided by enlightened self-interest, founded on psychic sagacity.

• • •

---

200   Stella Stuart. Quote continues "Why should I fear?" Quote appears in *Junior Republic* Volume 3 (1913).

The Source of Riches is Within

The source of all riches is within. There is no more difficulty in becoming rich than there is in becoming clever in a business or profession, only some men find the secret more easily than others.

Adverse circumstances never yet held down a man who was determined to rise. The more insuperable the difficulties the more powerful has the man become who has emerged from them. All the enemies a man has to contend with are of his own creation. One by one he can vanquish them if he will.

What man has done man can do.

What is the one desideratum in the acquirement of wealth? Talent? Not exactly. Some very talented men have been very poor. Education? No, there are plenty of educated men miserably poor. Trust in ourselves must come first. After that all is secondary. This is the common asset of every wealthy man. Luck, fate, chance, opportunity, have no claim to consideration. All of us, with very few exceptions, are psychologized by them. Opportunity, surely, you may say, plays some part? Contrast these two opinions respecting opportunity. The first you are probably familiar with, but the second is not so well known:

> Master of human destinies am I,
> Fame, love, and fortune on my footsteps wait.
> Cities and fields I walk; I penetrate
> Deserts and seas remote, and passing by
> Hovel, and mart, and palace—soon or late
> I knock unbidden once at every gate.
> If sleeping, wake—if feasting, rise before
> I turn away. It is the hour of fate,

And they who follow me reach every state
Mortals desire, and conquer every foe
Save death: but those who doubt or hesitate,
Condemned to failure, penury, and woe
Seek me in vain and uselessly implore -
I answer not, and I return no more.[201]

Here is the second:

They do me wrong who say I come no more
When once I knock and fail to find you in;
For every day I stand outside your door,
And bid you wake, and rise to fight and win.
Wail not for precious chances passed away,
Weep not for golden ages on the wane;
Each night I burn the records of the day,
At sunrise every soul is born again.
Dost thou behold thy lost youth all aghast?
Dost reel from righteous retribution's blow?
Then turn from blotted archives of the past,
And find the future's pages white as snow.
Art thou a mourner? Rouse thee from thy spell;
Art thou a sinner? Sins may be forgiven;
Each morning gives thee wings to flee from hell,
Each night a star to guide thy feet to heaven!
Laugh like a boy at splendours that have sped,
To vanished joys be blind and deaf and dumb;
My judgments seal the dead past with its dead,
But never bind a moment yet to come.
Though deep in mire, wring not your hands and weep;
I lend my arm to all who say: "I can."
No shamefaced outcast ever sank so deep
But yet might rise and be again a man.[202]

---

201   John James Ingalls (1833 - 1900). "Opportunity" from *Yale Book of American Verse* (1912).
202   Walter Malone (1866 - 1915). "Opportunity" from *The Little Book of American Poets 1787 -
1900* (1915).

A Rhapsody on Laughter

Laughter is an internal verity, and an external reality.

Laughter is the aftermath of the birth of mirth.

Brethren and co-workers in the vineyard of virolized vibrations! I purpose exposing thought-throbs, or mentoidal murmurings, for your mental mastication on the subject and object of Laughter.

Thomas Hobbes says: "There is a passion that hath no name, but the sign of it is that distortion of the countenance which we call laughter, which is always joy, but the Nature or cause of that joy nobody has explained."[203]

Whatever it be that moveth laughter, it must be new and unexpected. Man is the only animal that can laugh heartily, artfully, artlessly and artistically. The golden laughter of the philosopher, and the hearty laughter of the honest toiler are the two finest manifestations of mentoidal motion and ecstatic emotion in this world of commotion. "By their laughs ye shall know men."[204] Laughter is the lotion that lubricates the love of life, and lengthens the life of love.

As the sun colours the flowers, so laughter colours life. Laughter is the essence of enjoyment; the echo of ecstasy; the privilege of the poor; the perquisite of personality; the treasure of the toiler; the wealth of the wise, the truth of youth, and the head on the Bowl of Bliss.

If you wish to live 100 years begin today to laugh—and laugh until your heart is warm, and overflowing with vibrations of vitality and victorious vivacity; for laughter is the yeast of feeling; the feast of faith; the festoon of thought; and festival of

---

203   Quote from "Human Nature, or the Fundamental Elements of Policie" (1650).
204   In Matthew 7:16 it reads: "Ye shall know them by their fruits. Do men gather grapes of thorns, or figs of thistles?"

good fellowship; and the foam of the fountain of fancy.

Express happiness and you will attract it. The more you give out, the more comes back. You happiness is not in the hands of others, but is in you. Circumstances, environment, conditions, obstacles, and oppositions—all bow in complete obedience before the miracle force of laughter—for laughter is lord of levity and grand-master of gravity; when reinforced by the wizard of wisdom. Aerate your senses with the oxygen of laughter.

The lamps of laughter will lighten the path that leads to paradise. Happiness is the halo of humor; and humor the generator of laughter. The octaves of humor are as wide as human Nature. You can begin its cultivation anytime and anywhere. Humor purifies every hearthstone, creates domestic harmony, unshadows the brow of care, and spreads bountifully those rich graces which makes the world less sad. Humor makes for harmony—and harmony makes you likable, lovable, and sociable in character and conduct. Harmony checks discord in the mind, in the body, and in business.

Laughter mutilates morbidity, macerates malice, minimizes misery, and magnifies mercy. It is an anodyne for anguish, an iodyne for anger, an emulsion for envy. It is the solace of sorrow, the gleam in the golden glance, and the shimmer in the sunbeam of self-satisfaction. Laughter warms the cockles of the heart, invigorates the brain, purifies the blood, aids digestion, strengthens the nerves, and makes you feel as if you had money in the Bank of Bliss.

Arouse yourself! Express the divine desires and miracle of mirth within you. Know yourself from within, and you will better understand things from within. Quit contentions, bickerings, vain discussions, quarrels, strifes, and express happiness. Enjoy yourself while alive; for you will be long in the Tomb of Time. Move forward out of the fog of fear. Express enlightened ecstasy, tinctured by toleration; in your words; in your letters; in your manner; in your work; in your ideals; in your friendships;

in your kindness; in your beliefs. Radiate reason and happiness. Don't rupture a Rhapsody. Manipulate mirth by giving it away to your poor relations; for what you give to the poor you'll get back one-hundred fold.

Become a joy manufacturer. Wholesale and retail! Give away your joys; your griefs will take care of themselves. Become the incarnation of happiness. Let it be the atmosphere of your life. You will do it by thinking. Happiness is thought created. By thought you invoke, evolve, and produce happiness and laughter. Appeal to the Divinity that is within, and upon the invisible framework of your thoughts will the temple of your happiness be reared—and expressed—by laughter.

Laughter makes Kings envy peasants; plutocrats envy the poor; and the guilty envy the innocent.

So laugh and grow garrulous, genial, and generous in spirit and in deed, and you will become wealthy with wisdom, rich in reason, and opulent with optimism.

As Chamfort says: "The most wasted of all days is that on which one has not laughed. If your life is dull, brighten it with laughter; for laughter means strength, confidence and victory."[205]

A person who does not laugh is not healthy. Ironic, sardonic and sarcastic laughter is conterfeit laughter. It is laughter struggling to escape from the chains of chagrin and conceit. It is laughter in pain—striving to be itself again.

Thousands of nervous troubles would disappear if the human family cultivated the art of healthful buoyant laughter. Dyspepsia is on the increase where laughter is on the decrease. Where there is a famine of laughter, there can be found freaks with feculent frenzies, fanatics with false formulas, and rainbow chasers with stale shibboleths. Laughter is sound sublime and noise benign. It is noise in its most harmonious mood; a mood of matter mixed with mentality. It is the melody of matter, the music of motion, the mascot of mood and the monarch of mer-

205   Quote from "Maximes et Pensées" (1805) reads: "La plus perdue de toutes les journées est celle où l'on n'a pas ri."

riment; for it dispels dejection; destroys despair; banishes the blues, and mangles melancholia.

Laughter will reduce your blood pressure. Will ease the ill-humors of your body; for, it is the purloiner of pain; the policeman of passion; the sheriff of sorrow; the thief of grief; the foe of woe; the funeral of a frown, and the sheen on the soul of sound. If you desire the power of joy—laugh—loud and long. It's good for the lungs and the heart. Laughter has changed the bitter cup of tears into the mellow wine of wit and wisdom.

You can change the face of the world by laughter. The miracle of happiness is a Natural tonic that sets into exhilarating vibration myriads of sparkling joys. Laughter is medicine for the mind; the magician of social motion; and the equalizer of egoistic commotion in an ocean of emotion. Laughter is the sauce of self-satisfaction; the condiment of contentment; the consomme of consciousness, and the fizz in the froth of fun and fancy.

Laughter oils the wheels of the world and drives away miseries as the sun does the mist in the valley. Laughter assists the election of ecstasy to assassinate the atom of agony, and helps the molecule of mirth to murder the microbe of misery, while the mentoid of mercy smiles serenely upon the scene, with applause and approbation.

Laughter is the dimple of desire; the ripple of reason; the ragtime of reality; the sizzle of sanity; the vibrations of vanity; the pith of pleasure; the murmur of mirth, and the generator of the glands of gladness.

Without laughter life would be livid with lawless wrath, humor would be a tumor on the tongue of truth; and a blister on the bosom of bliss; wit would be weird and weary; smiles would shiver with sheer shame; dimples would depart for other parts; for laughter is the voice of a clear conscience, the glow of a clear concept; the simmer of a sincere soul; the birth mark of mirth; the magic of matter; the halo of happiness and the "swan-song of sadness."

What Is Man?

Average man weighs 154 pounds.

WHAT MEN ARE MADE OF?

A notable object of interest is described as among the contents of the National Museum, Washington, showing the ingredients which go to make up the average man, weighing 154 pounds. A large glass jar holds the ninety-six pounds of water which his body contains, while in other receptacles three pounds of "white of egg," a little less than ten pounds of pure glue, thirty-four and one-half pounds of fat, eight and one-fourth pounds of phosphate of lime, one pound carbonate of lime, three ounces of sugar and starch, seven ounces fluoride of calcium, six ounces phosphate of magnesium, and a little ordinary table salt. The same man is found to contain ninety-seven pounds of oxygen, fifteen pounds of hydrogen, three pounds and thirteen ounces of nitrogen, and the carbon in such an individual is represented by a foot cube of coal. A row of bottles contain the other elements going to make up the man; these being four ounces of chlorine, three and one-half ounces fluorine, eight ounces phosphorus, three and one-half ounces of brimstone, two and one-half ounces each of sodium and potassium, one-tenth of an ounce of iron, two ounces magnesium, three pounds and three ounces of calcium.

POINTS OF INTEREST ABOUT
THE HUMAN BODY

In the human body there are about two hundred and sixty-three bones. The muscles are about five hundred in number.

The length of the alimentary canal is about thirty-two feet.

The amount of blood in an adult averages thirty pounds, or fully one-fifth of the entire weight.

The heart is about four inches in diameter and about six inches in length, beating seventy times a minute, four thousand and two hundred times an hour, one hundred thousand eight hundred times a day, and over thirty-six million times a year. At each beat of the heart over two ounces of blood is thrown out of it, one hundred and eighty ounces a minute, six hundred pounds an hour, and about eight tons per day.

All the blood in the body passes through the heart in three minutes.

This little organ by its ceaseless industry, pumps each day what is equal to lifting one hundred and thirty tons one foot high, or one ton one hundred and thirty feet high.

The lungs contain about one gallon of air at their usual degree of inflation.

We breath, on an average, one thousand two hundred time an hour, inhale six hundred gallons of air, or thirty-four thousand quarts a day. The aggregate surface of the air cells of the lungs exceeds twenty thousand square inches. The average weight of the brain of an adult male is three pounds and eight ounces; of a female two pounds and four ounces.

The nerves probably exceed ten million in number.

The skin is composed of three layers and varies from one-eighth to one-quarter of an inch in thickness.

As William James says: "The ideal of the well-trained and vigorous body should be maintained neck by neck with that of the well-trained and vigorous mind." And the only way of accomplishing this result is by letting food science, exercise, etc., go hand in hand with the wonderful science of mind. Thus alone may we attain and maintain perfect health and supreme mental efficiency."[206]

---

206   William James (1842 - 1910). Psychologist. Quote from *The Gospel of Relaxation* (1922).

How many of us, I wonder, can say truthfully, "I am 100 percent efficient. My brain is always clear. My body is in perfect health. I start my day's work with a feeling of buoyancy, and at the day's close I am as full of vitality and brain force as when I began."

Yet, unless we enjoy perfect health like that we are not getting out of life the joys that should be ours—we are not making the most of our lives nor realizing our greatest possibilities.

The majority of us are not eager for big muscles and prodigious strength. Our daily occupations do not require the physique of a Hercules. But we need bodies and brains so efficient and in such smooth running order that our daily tasks may be performed joyously without fatigue and without brain fag.

We want health, strength and vitality because we realize they are essential to our success and happiness. How may we attain them best?

Of course, every reader knows that the mind exerts control over every action and every process of the body, and that even the involuntary muscles which move the heart, lungs, stomach, kidneys, liver, etc., and the nerves which direct their functions are controlled by the mind through the subconscious part of our being which works through the brain, the spinal cord and the solar plexus.

The mind is the fountain head of human energy, but we must also develop muscular and nervous strength by judicious exercise, by proper breathing, by the right diet best suited to our individual requirements, and by living common sense lives in accordance with Nature's laws. We must combine true physical culture and food science with a knowledge of the laws of practical psychology, and thus, by training our mental and physical forces simultaneously we may attain complete harmony of mind and body, and the result will be maximum efficiency of body and brain.

Remember, your body is maintained through a process of continuous destruction and reconstruction. Life is simply an exchange of the old for the new, and health is only the equilibrium which Nature maintains during the process of creating new tissue and eliminating the old or waste tissue. Birth and death are constantly taking place in our body, new cells are constantly being formed by the process of converting food, water and air into living tissue. Every action of the brain, every movement of a muscle means the destruction and consequent death of some of these cells and the accumulation of these dead, unused and waste cells are the causes of pain, suffering and disease.

• • •

THE AMBROSIAL FOOD OF THE GODS

On rising, take a glass of fruit-liquor, the juices of lemon and orange mixed.

For breakfast: Take one pint of lukewarm milk into which put a good eating apple, cut into small pieces. Let it rest until a curd arises then eat slowly.

Afterward eat a mutton chop with whole wheat bread. Masticate well. Drink no liquor while eating.

Healthful emotions simulate while destructive emotions inhibit and destroy.

THE RIGHT WAY TO BREATHE

Correct breathing is a most important function of the body, and a great preventative of disease, especially lung trouble. Many people make the mistake of breathing only with the upper part of the lungs instead of the whole.

All singers who are taught correct breathing pay special attention to this point, but it is one which should be appreciated by every woman who values her health.

When practicing this exercise discard all tight-fitting garments, stand erect out of doors, or indoors in a well-ventilated room, clasp the lower part of the ribs with a hand on each side. the tips of the fingers lightly touching. Do not raise the shoulders, but take a slow, deep breath until the lungs are filled—that is until no more air can be taken in comfortably. There must be no forcing or exaggeration in this exercise; hold the breath for three seconds, and then exhale, gently and evenly.

• • •

A "Dizzy" Sensation

The breath must not be held too long, or the exercise repeated more than half a dozen times consecutively at first. Beginners sometimes feel a sensation of dizziness, but this will gradually pass as they become accustomed to using their lungs properly.

Children and grown-ups should practice correct breathing. It purifies and enriches the blood, consequently improving the complexion. The benefit in the general health is often remarkable.

STANDARD HEALTH RULES

To attain health and keep it, to prevent disease and eradicate it, Nature provided a few simple rules which are not only to be known but must be observed if life is to prove a state of joy and success:

1. Never use fruits and vegetables at the same meal.
2. Select your food according to the productions of the season.
3. For the first meal of the day or breakfast, use fresh fruits or fruit juices, whatever of the local market or imported, adding rolled oats, wheat or rice.
4. For the second meal of the day, or lunch, have a salad, toast or any wholesome unfermented bread.
5. For the third meal use seasonable appetizers, such as diverse melons, cucumbers or gourds in general, and in their ab-

sence whatever salad are procurable, like tomatoes, endives, celery, chicory, chives, green onions, leeks, kale, cabbage, lettuce, fennels, sorrel, watercress, radishes, carrots, beets, and turnips, the three later being available at any time. In addition to fresh appetizers use any vegetable, or vegetables, suitable for baking or steaming in their own juice, using absolutely no water in preparing such dishes, adding olive, sunflower, coconut, peanut, corn or cooking oil to avoid scorching, and steam over a slow fire. Fresh biscuits or yeast-free breadstuffs may be added to suit the taste, although raw cereals are preferred.

In addition to the above five rules, the following should be observed to hasten results and derive benefits, other than those of physical merit.

6. Select your fruits, salad stuffs, vegetables, grains, nuts, dairy and yard products according to temperament and basic principles.
7. The intellectually based need largely stone and seedless fruits (mostly tropical), salads, baked vegetables, almonds, pistachios and cashews. Should use very little yard or dairy food and seldom drink with meals. Milk and butter conceded.
8. The spiritually based need seed fruits, mostly semi-tropical, more salads, steam and baked vegetables, uncooked, rolled and crushed grains, pine nuts, brazils, peanuts, barn products in season, also dairy food in season, thoroughly cured cheese with lemon juice in season and in small quantities, black tea and coffee, altho seldom with meals.
9. The physically based can have all the domestic fruits, less of the tropical or semi-tropical unless for remedial purposes. Plenty of salads, raw, steamed, baked, fried and stewed vegetables, raw and cooked cereals, unfermented bread dairy and yard

foods in season, walnuts, pecans and peanuts. They should drink before meals, but not with or immediately after them.

• • •

If you are unhappy don't blame others, for your trouble is the result of your own thoughts.

If you exercise your thought powers aright no matter what others might think, say or do, you would enjoy perfect peace, health, and happiness. Most people in this world are about as happy as they have made up their minds to be.

Sickness is due primarily to wrong thinking. Failure is caused by the negative aspect of thought power.

Positive thought is uplifting, fearless, confident and causes good effects, to sender and receiver.

Negative thought is uncertain: Selfish, weak and works bad for all. It has been claimed that emotions cause the secretion of definite chemical substances, which can partly be expelled by the breath; various emotions cause different colored precipitates in a given solution. There is no question of the beneficial effects of healthful emotions and the detrimental effects of the reverse. It is not so much the effects of the thought upon the body as the emotion aroused by and associated with the thought. Practically all emotions give rise to bodily expression. Darwin wrote an extensive monograph upon *The Expression of the Emotions in Men and Animals*.

Fear, anger, and hate find visible expression in the face and in the actions of the body. These and envy, malice, jealousy, etc., affect the blood stream.

To succeed is to have courage and self-control, to be strong and sturdy, to think fast and act quickly, to be married happily, to be immune from sickness, consider your diet.

All life is a battle for place—the fittest only stay alive. What you eat and what you think determines your fitness to fight and conquer in life's battles.

• • •

DRY FEEDING

It is against Nature to eat and drink at meals.

It is against Nature to mix varieties of food at the same meal. Dry feeding is based on common sense. As a rule, frugvorous animals confine themselves to fruit, the carnivorous to meat, and several feeders to grain, while the omnivorous exercise a discretion which should shame civilized man in his efforts to commit racial suicide.

The claims and advantages of dry feeding are easily explained. Digestion can be properly performed only by an efficient condition of the salivary and gastric juices. Let sloppy foods be eaten and beverages be mixed with meals, and the gastric functions become weakened, and perhaps, in the end disorganized by dilution. The gastric juices are the Natural food-dissolvents, and with most of us those dissolvents are weakened by our erring habits in eating and drinking.

We are told that the blood stream makes a complete circuit of the human structure once in every four minutes, or three hundred and sixty times a day, permeating and influencing the extremest parts of the body. Not a particle of us can escape its influence for our physical good or harm. Hence the vast importance of our state of blood in the determination of health and sickness. Do we think of that fact—do we realize its tremendous issues—while we poison our bodies with ill-chosen food and drink, and the drugs we take make bad worse?

Fruit juice—as contained in lemons, oranges and grapes—is a potent cleanser of the blood, which, by reaction, is rendered alkaline. Let the power of this purifying agency he recognized—emphasized, as it is, 360 times a day in the circulation of the blood—and the secret of my convictions will be easily understood.

The effects of fruit juice are amazing. A friend took lemon

juice to cure rheumatism, and her bunions disappeared; while another, with the same purpose, discovered a cure for varicose veins, after wearing bandages for more than twenty years. And why not? If deadly poison will kill almost on the instant, the process is the same in its action on the blood. Be assured that fruit juice will course through the frame as rapidly as beer or whiskey.

Assume that today an administration of the fruit juice has been made—say that a pint of lemon and orange juice has been absorbed—and the reactive influence referred to is at once communicated to the blood-stream. The transition begins with the first dose, and within a week or two a marked change has been established in the constitution of the frame—bones, tissue, nails, eyes; every organ and function of the body is better for it.

This alteration in the blood (and consequent change in the whole frame) is speedily manifested in a pause in the growth and development of the disease, whether the cancer be internal or external; though, if external, the cancer has the additional chance of subjugation through the bathing of the wound with lemon juice.

Why? Because the clean blood builds; the medicine is food—food possessed of life elements in itself, just as the blood is the life, so is it life which makes the pure blood. Life must be fed with life; do not the flesh-eating animals prefer the living flesh? Chemical remedies, so-called, are absolutely different. They are dead in themselves; they do not remove the cause, and thereby they fail. The new blood makes a new body; not slowly, but with marvelous rapidity. Brick by brick the structure is re-made, as it were, and new pure tissue takes the place of the old foul tissue.

To make the fruit-liquor: Take a heaped tablespoonful of currants, sultanas, or raisins (best quality); place in a colander and stream under the cold water tap for a moment, to clean; then place in a cup and add two tablespoonfuls of cold water and the juice of half a lemon. Let stand overnight, and on rising sip the liquor, afterwards thoroughly masticating the whole or part of the remaining fruit. For a family, of course, make proportionately more. There will be no constipation in the home where the fruit-liquor is systematically taken; the results are worth the little trouble of preparation. An action of the bowels will generally be induced before breakfast—a desirable habit to acquire. For infants give a teaspoonful, and from one to two tablespoonfuls to children, according to age and judgment. For the peel-and-pip water: soak the peel and pips of oranges and lemons in cold water, overnight; the tonic properties, so extracted, are remarkable. Use plenty of water, and always cold— hot, or boiling, will spoil it. Honey is wonderfully feeding and purifying. It is practically all nourishment, and is almost immediately absorbed. Buy only the best quality obtainable.

Eat sparingly of the starchy foods—they constipate.

Be careful of the cream. Eggs, too, are potent food, to be given occasionally, not habitually, to children and delicate adults. I have discarded eggs.

All frying-pan food is indigestible. Bacon is gross; the nuts will take its place.

To lightly cook an egg, put it into about a pint of boiling water, then take the saucepan off the fire, and in about six minutes the egg will be congealed—but not killed.

THE LEMON CURE
By R. Mallet[207]

During the past ten years I have drawn attention to the virtues of lemon-juice as a remedy for the many ills which proceed from one root cause—namely, a vitiated condition of the blood.

To keep the blood pure is to do the best one can for the maintenance of good health; there is no surer armor against disease.

Healthy blood should have an alkaline tendency, and I have

---

207   Josiah Reddie Mallett (1864 - ?). Paraphrased from *Nature's Way* (1922).

proved by experiments upon my own body, as well as by an astonishing concurrence of testimony from other sources, that lemon-juice possesses, in its reactive properties, an unquestionable power to induce that state of alkalinity.

Lemon-juice is generally spoken of as acid, and no greater error has been entertained by those in search of health who, merely through ignorance, have allowed themselves to be prejudiced against this wonderful food-medicine.

Lemon-juice is acid to the tongue, it is true, and by its original elements it may be so classed; but as soon as it enters the system a remarkable change is wrought upon its chemical composition, due to the action of the digestive process.

By that process acid becomes alkaline, and sweet becomes sour, for in the latter instance how often is it noticed that sugar in one's tea will aggravate an attack of biliousness.

A short trial will place the purifying qualities of lemon-juice beyond dispute. There will quickly come a feeling of freshness to the whole body, the blood is being cleansed. The frame will be warmed by the removal of the poisons which have clogged the organs. More muscular power will be given to every limb, and more alertness to the mind, because functions and senses are being freed from the burdens which brought lethargy and depression. Lemon-juice will clean the frame from the soles of the feet to the crown of the head—even the eyesight is improved by this marvelous cordial—and they will be happier homes in which it is habitually taken as an important part of the daily dietary. Most of us suffer from gastric troubles; lemon-juice is the cure. Nearly every one is a prey to worms, children being by no means the only sufferers. and lemon-juice will speedily rid the intestines of those debilitating parasites. Lemon-juice will cure piles; while boils, sores, and wounds will promptly yield to the magic of this Natural disinfectant. It will cure rheumatism, gout, asthma, and bronchitis. It will break down diabetes by changing the character of the blood. It is the cure for influenza, catarrh, and all inflammatory troubles. It will bring new life to the anaemic and the vitally weak; it is advised by me in cases of cancer and consumption. Were its manifold purposes properly understood, how soon would the wailing of sickly children be assuaged, how gladly would men and women meet the labor of the day!

• • •

FOOD AS MEDICINE
Compiled from data provided by the U. S. Government.
Dr. Harvey M. Wiley says:
"Food will be the medicine of the future."[208]

ALMONDS—Very fine for the Muscles, Brain and Nerves. Nuts are a very powerful food and should be either eaten alone between meals or with fresh fruit.

APPLES—One of the finest fruits in the world. Beneficial for Biliousness, Constipation, Acidity, Gout, Jaundice, Indigestion, Liver Trouble, Nervousness, Skin Disease and Sleeplessness.

APRICOTS—Especially good for Worms and Consumption.

ARTICHOKES—Good for Dropsy and Jaundice. Contain much Iron.

ASPARAGUS—Cleans out the Lungs and Kidneys. Good for Asthma, Consumption and Bright's Disease. Easy to digest.

BEETS—Aid Indigestion and all Stomach Troubles. Good for Erysipelas, Jaundice and Skin Diseases of all kinds.

CABBAGE—Good for Skin Diseases and Blood Diseases. Anti-Scorbutic. Good for Asthma, Gout, Scurvy, also for the Nails, Teeth and Hair.

CARROTS—Especially good for the Complexion and Hair— also a wonderful relief for Nervousness.

CAULIFLOWER—Good for the same things as Cabbage.

CELERY—This is a brain food. Good for Neuralgia, Rheuma-

---

208   Harvey Washington Wiley (1844 - 1930). Chemist. Quote from *The Department of Agriculture Report of the Women's Institutes of the Province of Ontario* (1919).

tism, Skin Diseases, Gout, Liver and Kidney Trouble.

CHERRIES—Very good for Bright's Disease.

COCOANUT—A very nutritious food. Cocoanut milk is good for Fever and Exhaustion and the ground fresh nut and mixed with its own milk will expel Tapeworms.

CRANBERRIES—Good for Liver Trouble, Kidney Trouble, Skin Diseases; and Cranberry Juice makes an excellent drink in Fevers.

CUCUMBERS—Very good for the Complexion and all Skin Diseases.

CURRANTS—Currant Beverage is especially good in Fevers. Also good for Coughs and Colds. Also Sore Throat.

DANDELlON—Good for Dyspepsia, Liver and Kidney Troubles, Skin and Blood Diseases, Ague, Bright's Disease.

DATES—Especially rich in Vitamins. Good for Circulation and supply much necessary heat to the body.

ELDERBERRIES—Good for Sore Throat, Coughs and Colds.

ENDIVE—Good for Skin Diseases, Liver and Kidney Troubles.

FENNEL—Good for Spleen and Gall Troubles as well as Skin Diseases and Liver Trouble.

FIGS—A very fine food containing much nutrition. Good for Liver Trouble and Constipation, also all Skin Diseases and the Blood.

GARLIC—A very healthful food in spite of its odor. Very good for Blood and Skin Diseases.

GOOSEBERRIES—Fine for Liver, Kidney and Stomach Disorders.

GRAPES—Especially good as they contain most of the Mineral Salts. Good for Blood and Skin Diseases, Consumption, Dyspepsia, Indigestion, Fevers, Liver and Kidney Troubles.

HONEY—One of the best concentrated foods known. Easy to digest. Good for Throat and Lung Affections, also for Kidney and Bladder disorders. Is a Natural Laxative and sedative. This should be used instead of white sugar as it is an organic food.

HORSERADISH—Good for Asthma, Dropsy, Rheumatism, Catarrh and all Skin Diseases. Good for Liver and Spleen.

LETTUCE—Very rich in Iron. Good for Sleeplessness or Insomnia, Stomach disorders, Indigestion, Dyspepsia, etc.

MELONS—All kinds of Melons are excellent for the Kidneys and the Liver. A Natural Laxative.

OLIVE OIL—It is very lubricating, which makes it invaluable for Constipation and Indigestion. Good for Skin Diseases.

OLIVES—An especially nutritious food. It cleans, beautifies and rejuvenates the entire system.

ONlONS—Wonderful for the Blood and Skin. They cleanse the system. Good for Sleeplessness, Nervousness, Coughs and Colds.

ORANGES, LEMONS AND GRAPEFRUIT—These fruits all belong to the same family and are the best of all fruits. They are especially strong in Vitamins and supply those which are missing from the Pasteurized milk. Very strongly anti-scorbutic with strong tonic properties. Good for all Skin and Blood Diseases and will prevent Scurvy. A glass of Orange juice and Grapefruit juice mixed is one of the best things you can take the first thing every morning—it will preserve your health and help you keep young.

PARSLEY—Good for Bright's Disease, Gallstones, Dropsy, Kidney and Liver Trouble, Venereal Diseases and Enlarged Glands.

PARSNIPS—They are very good for Dyspepsia.

PEANUTS, BRAZIL NUTS—All nuts are very Fattening.

PEACHES—Especially good for Worms and Consumption.

PEARS—A Natural laxative when eaten very ripe.

POMEGRANATES—Good for Coughs, Colds, Sore Throat, Lung Troubles, Hemorrhages and Tape Worms.

PRUNES—One of the most valuable foods known to man, containing practically all of the Mineral Salts and much nutrition, they rebuild the body and regulate the Bowels, a Natural Laxative.

QUINCES—A Natural Laxative, good in all Stomach and Bowel Disorders and help stop Vomiting.

RADISHES—Contain many of the Mineral Salts and are a very useful Appetizer.

RAISINS—Contain all the good qualities of the original Grapes and the action of the sun has made them much richer in Sugar in its organic form. A very fine food.

RASPBERRIES—Good for Cholera, Sore Throat and Fevers.

RHUBARB—Use this in place of Vinegar which is indigestible. A very fine eliminator and good for Cancer.

SAGE—Good for Lung Trouble, Piles, Rheumatism.

SALT—Not a food in any way. Too much salt will cause Trouble.

SPINACH—Good for Heart Disease, Piles, Stomach Trouble, Skin and Blood Diseases.

STRAWBERRIES—Especially good in Skin Diseases. If they cause rash to break out that shows you need them. Also good for Acne, Gout and Ringworm.

TOMATOES—Both a fruit and a vegetable and rank next to the orange in high value. Wonderful Kidney and Liver remedy. Good for Dyspepsia and Stomach Inflammations. Contains the Vitamins that are lacking in Pasteurized milk. Either Orange juice or Tomato juice are necessary for young children.

TURNIPS—Good for Ulcers of the Bladder and Skin Diseases. They contain much necessary Calcium for the teeth and bones.

WATERCRESS—One of the best Blood cleansers known. Good for all Stomach, Liver and Kidney Troubles as well as Skin Diseases. A very good Brain and Nerve food as well.

SIXTEEN ELEMENTS CONTAINED IN VARIOUS FOODS

(And the amount of each contained in a person weighing 150 lbs.)

When we analyze the human body, we find that, like the soil and the plant, it is made up principally of the following sixteen elements:

OXYGEN (97 lbs., 12 oz.). In all foods—both good and bad. (Air.)

HYDROGEN (ll lbs., 12 oz.). In all foods—good and bad. (Water.)

NITROGEN (2 lbs., 14 oz.). Especially rich in all nuts. In air and water.

CARBON (30 lbs.). In fresh, uncooked fruits and vegetables, air and water.

CALCIUM (2 lbs.). Spinach, Beets, Oats, Whole Wheat, Whole Rye, Beans, Carrots, Meat, Potatoes, Radishes, Onions, Garlic, Rhubarb, Fruits.

IRON (180 grns.). Whole Wheat, Oats and Rye, Beans, Spinach, Carrots, Fruits, Parsnips, Meat, Potatoes, Eggs, Cabbage, Milk, Nuts, Raisins.

IODIN (Very small). Sea Food, Onions, Garlic, Citrus Fruits, Tomatoes, Barnes, Eggs, Grapes and Artichokes.

CHLORINE (2 02., 250 grns.). Fresh Uncooked Vegetables. Milk. Egg Yolk.

SULPHUR (3 02., 270 grns.). Cabbage, Onions, Garlic, Radishes, Raw Eggs.

FLUORINE (215 grns.). All Whole Grain Foods, Fresh Leafy Vegetables, Milk, Onions, Garlic, Greens, Cabbage, Lettuce.

PHOSPHORUS (11b., 12 oz., 190 grns.). Milk, Carrots, Chestnuts, Cheese, Beef, Turnips, Spinach, Cabbage, Eggs, Whole Grains, Parsnips, Radishes, Baked Potatoes, Cottage

Cheese, Citrus Fruits, Lettuce, Nuts.

POTASSIUM (290 grns.). Veal, Eggs, Potatoes, Milk, Peas, Carrots, Radishes, Whole Grains, Spinach. Parsnips, Beans, Peas, Cottage Cheese, Nuts, Asparagus, Apples, Figs, Prunes, Dates and Berries.

SODIUM (2 02., 196 grns.). Eggs, Potatoes, Beans. Milk. Carrots, Peas, Veal, Parsnips, Radishes, Whole Grains, Spinach, Peaches, Figs, Celery, Nuts.

MAGNESIUM (340 grns.). Citrus Fruits, Apples, Cherries, Grapes, Nuts, Peaches, Whole Grains, Milk, Greens.

SILICON (116 grns.). Whole Grains, Eggs, Berries, Peaches, Cherries, Grapes, Greens, Spinach, Cabbage, Carrots, Radishes, Beans.

MANGANESE (90 gms.). Sea Foods, Nuts and Greens.

• • •

"Search in, search out, and 'round about,
The Truth is the same forever.
Of this there is no shadow of doubt,
No probable, possible shadow of doubt,
No possible doubt whatever."

"Sip no longer from the saucer of sorrow,
But drink from the bowl of bliss
Until the juice of joy comes forth from
Every proud and puissant pore, galore,
With an encore—and some more."

A Supercrat is an Ego on The Full-Shell.

"In the Tomb of Time we wander,
In the Womb of Wisdom we wonder,
In the Shades of Space we slumber,
In the Meadows of Meditation we meander."

Some spend their nights in the Region of Romance, others spend their days in the Realm of Reason as they walk down the Avenue of Adventure along the Pathway of Progress that leads to the Millennium, where Peace, Plenty, Power and Personalities abound and no Cheap Organisms are allowed around, for, when found, they find the Ground with Solid Sound, and are never more seen in that Town.

The Egocrat will help the Molecule of Mirth to murder the Microbe of Misery and assist the Electron of Ecstasy to assassinate the Atom of Agony, while the Mentoid of Mercy gazes upon the sightly scene with appreciation and applause.

WHAT IS A SIRFESSOR?

A heckler asked this question of Malfew Seklew.
This was the answer: A Sirfessor is a Knight of Knowledge amongst benighted bipeds who peddle pestiferous piffle. A Supercrat of Sanity offering a salve for the woes of humanity.

• • •

The Society of Social Supercrats

It Affirms That:

All progress is aristocratic, individualistic, and egoistic, fundamentally, and collective, incidentally.

Progress is the past and present—plus the future made by the unique ego with intuition, imitation and imagination. First, psychologization, visualization, materialization and realization.

Advocates:

Stirpiculture[209]—The Science of a New Life.
Mindology or Mentology—The Science of a New Mind.
Superology—The Science of a New System.

• • •

Be a Social Aristocrat and Join the Aristocracy of aim, action and ambition.

• • •

This Society was founded in England in 1897, in Scotland in 1906, in Chicago in 1916, and in New York in 1918.[210]

• • •

F. M. WILKESBARR, President.
A. SAGE, Secretary.
MALCOLM COLE, Treasurer.
Address: 923 N. La Salle St., Chicago, 111., U. S. A.
Telephone: Diversey 4333.

• • •

Join the Fesserhood—The first degree of the Order of Social Supercrats.

---

209   John Humphrey Noyes (1811 - 1886). Utopian. Coined the phrases "free love" and "stirpiculture."
210   In 1897, Sirfessor Wilkesbarre was 33 years old and lived in Manchester and Lancashire, England. Wilkesbarre moved in Chicago Illinois in 1916.

Join the Egohood—The second degree of the Order.
Join the Superhood—The third degree of the Order.

• • •

Become an Ego Conscious 100 percent Personality, and you will become wealthy with wisdom, rich in reason, and opulent with optimism.

• • •

Can you crucify your conscience on the cross of consciousness or Fletcherize your frenzies, Borrilize your beliefs, Pasteurize your prejudices, Burbankize your beatitudes, Bowlerize your banalities, virilize your vibrations, audit your own agonies, and paralyze your own paralogie, while you manufacture your own mirth, mollity your own misery, and emulsify your own malice? Can you pulverize your own piffle, sterilize your own slogan or stale shibboleths, and mesmerize your own melancholy? It you can, you are an Egocrat *in excelsis* and *a ram avis* among men, an ego on the full-shell, an entity with an identity, a personality with a punch, and individuality with an insight into life, surpassing all others. If not, join the Order.

• • •

Learn How To Psychologize

Egos Vivisected While You Wait.

Bon Mots bought and sold.

Epigrams exchanged and repaired while you wait.

Wit washed and renovated.

Reason radiumized.

Metaphors mended and defended.

Solecisms soled and heeled.

Shibboleths shattered and scattered.

Paradoxes prepared and protected.

Principles preserved and embalmed in the latest style.

Platitudes from any latitude reduced to brevity and sanity.

Sobs sorted and strangled to order.

Sorrow sequestered and segregated.

Thought transformed into truth and truth made triumphant,
   reinforced by reason and righteousness.

Egos examined and explained.

Individuality identified and rectified.

Personality provided with a punch.

Characters classified and codified.

Thoughts incubated and reorganized.

Desire dissected, Reason resurrected, Vibrations vivisected.

Hate humiliated and humanized.

Vanity sanitized.

Sanity vanitized with victory.

Success secured and sustained.

Master Minds manufactured to order.

Highbrows anointed with Haloes.

Lowbrows scolded and remoulded.

Delusions ravished with reason.

Illusions illustrated by ridicule.

The Gospel According to Malfew Seklew

Your Ego Examined and Explained

Brain-throbs captured and embalmed.

Learn how to measure your own misery, and weigh your own wisdom.

Agonies Audited.

Motives massaged.

Mentoids manicured and manipulated.

Molecules of Mirth multiplied and supplied.

Epigrams and Epigrins to order.

Democracy dissected and demonetized.

Superstitions suffocated.

Prejudices paralyzed.

Paralogies pulverized.

Anger and Anguish analyzed and annihilated.

Preserved prejudices and pickled principles explained and ex-posed.

Proper pride made profitable.

Morbid moods mutilated or removed.

Fear frustrated.

Remorse removed by reason.

Bliss without blisters supplied.

Misery mesmerized.

Happiness harnessed with harmony.

Despair destroyed.

Courage encouraged.

Ignorance ignored.

Wisdom made welcome.

Desire directed with discretion.

Nightmares turned into horses of another color.

Dreams diagnosed.

Vice vivisected and redirected.

Truth made Triumphant.

Worry washed in the waters of wisdom.

Laughter located and supplied to order.

Vibrations virolized...

F. M. Wilkesbarr, S.S.M.M.—the Laughing Philosopher of Lancashire. Talkologist, Neologist, Mentoidologist, Stirpi-culturist and Neo-Psychological. Author of *Demi-Gods Demi-Damned, or Halo's Hoodooed*.

"Evangelist of *The Gospel According to Malfew Seklew*."

> "F. M. Wilkesbarr is the most original aboriginal and indi-vidual talkologist and jocular jawsmith that I ever heard in Hyde Park. He is the George Bernard Shaw of the 'Fo-rums' and a masterpiece of 'mentoidal murmurings.'"[211]
> —Lord Erwin McCall,
> Editor of *Eagle and Serpent*, London.

> "I have heard G. B. Shaw, G. K. Chesterton and others, but F. M. W., the Laughing Philosopher, surpasses them all as a maker of epigrams and epigrins."[212]
> —A. W. Haycock,
> Member of Parliament from North Salford, England.

> "He, F. M. W., stands alone as a unique Ego, as he dashes through space with a smile on his face."[213]
> —Joseph Toole,
> member of Parliament from South Salford, England.

F. M. Wilkesbarre, S.S.M.M., is prepared to give his lectures on "Laughter," "Love," "Men," "Women," "Wit and Wisdom of Malfew Seklew," etc., before Women's Clubs, Businessmen's Clubs, or elsewhere. (These lectures were given over the Radio in England.)

For terms apply to Secretary, 923 N. La Salle St., Chicago, Ill.

---

211   John Basil Barnhill aka John Erwin McCall (1864 - 1929). Editor, *The Eagle and The Serpent*.
212   Alexander Wilkinson Frederick Haycock (1882 - 1970). Politician.
213   Joseph Toole (1887 - 1945). Politician.

●●●

Are you a Simpoleon or a Supercrat? A Peter-pantheist or a Personality? Are you a Bromide or a Sulphide? A nonentity or a reality? Are you an unripe ego or an unfinished organism with underdone understanding and hard-boiled beliefs, pingpong principles and petrified prejudices? Do you amble through the atmosphere with the courage of a carrot, the consciousness of a cabbage, the turpitude of a turnip, the pep of a prune, the punch of a parsnip and the psychology of a Sundowner in the swamps of Hobohemia, or do you dash through space with the courage of a Conqueror and the wisdom of a Will-to-Power Man?

If not, massage your Mentoids, and be saved—from yourself at your worst.

F. M. WILKESBARR
Sirfessor of Superology and Mater of Mentoitlology
Gives Consultations Daily to all who wish to have their Character Classified, their Personality Peptonized, and their Ego Elevated and Cultivated.

You must be Egoized before you can be really civilized; and have your ideals realized.

Office hours: 11 A. M. to 8 P. M. at 923 N. La. Salle Street, Chicago, Ill.

Become an Ego Conscious, 100 percent Personality, and you will be rich in reason, wealthy with wisdom and opulent with optimism.

The DAY BOOK Debates

ONE CENT—LAST EDITION—ONE CENT

ALDERMEN TO BE FORCED OUT IN OPEN
INDICT OWNER OF MUNITION PLANT

THE DAY BOOK

An Adless Newspaper, Daily Except Sunday

VOL. 5, NO. 113   Chicago, Wednesday, February 9, 1916   398 ◄══════

GAS CONSUMERS HAVE CHANCE FOR REFUND

Richberg Renews Fight to Have $10,000,000 of People's Money Returned—Charges Company Inflates Plant Value to Boost Price of Gas.

Chicago is now paying 80 cents per thousand cubic feet for gas. This is an inflated price, for, according to the ordinance of 1911, the housewives should be paying 68 cents a thousand cubic feet. But the gas company got that ordinance enjoined by the court and they have gone on charging 80 cents for the past five years. The difference between the ordinance rate and that charged by the gas company was impounded. It has now reached the total of $10,-000,000.

Att'y Donald Richberg, who is fighting in court to get back this money for the city, told the Seventh Ward Open Forum at their meeting why the gas rate was so high. He charged that thirty years of mismanagement and dishonesty in public office had saddled upon the people the 80-cent rate they are now paying and that the enormous profits of the gas company go to pay dividends on $85,-000,000 worth of stocks and bonds which the public utilities commission has declared to be one-half water.

Cover of The Day Book, *published February 9th, 1916.*

Got Kibbler's Goat

The Day Book 21 January 1916.

A lecture delivered in room 811, Masonic Temple, has succeeded in getting my goat.

The speaker was a Mr. Wilkesbarre, who, by the way calls himself Prof. Wilkesbarre, and the subject was "Ego."

Among the many statements that got me were the following:

Socialism is a brain disease.

Self-preservation is not the first law of nature.

Exploitation is the first law of progress.

The first he backs up by saying that socialism is full of silly, sloppy sentiments, altruism and a pitiful plea for something that isn't there. The second by stating that if it was left to the working class we would have no progress, as it (the working class) only does as it is told, so therefore if not ordered it remains where it is.

In discussing the third point he said that self-realization, not self-preservation, is the first law. Then went on to say that only "cheap organisms," to use his own terms, are afraid of death, for "conscious egos," or "finished organisms," value their ideals more than life.

To my mind his first outburst demonstrates his ignorance of socialism. I would like him to meet some of our expounders of the cause. I do not think the capitalists would do much if left to themselves.

Mr. Wilkesbarre remarked that the working class was a mass of matter that did not matter and that the only thing it is good for is to go to work or to do as it is told.

He spoke before a large number of people and seemed to me to be full of the very thing he was speaking of, ego.

—W. Kibbler.

Who Can This Be?

The Day Book 27 January 1916.

A writer who frequently contributes articles to *The Day Book*, whose conceit, vanity and egoism is so deeply rooted that no amount of criticism, sarcasm or ridicule can eradicate it from his system, has seated himself upon the pedestal of supreme knowledge and has assumed the role of master educator to enlighten ignorant humanity. He imagines the public is vitally interested in all the rambling thoughts that percolates through his dizzy brain, none of which are of an educational feature. Apparently no amount of pressure can make him realize his incompetency to fill the role he has assumed. Now, all together, one big guess! Who is it?

—M. Rasmussen.

Knocks Socialism

The Day Book 27 January 1916.

Undoubtedly the lecture delivered by Sirfessor Wilkesbarre in Masonic Temple not only got Mr. Kibbler's goat, but according to his own writeup in The Public Forum it must have wrecked his nervous system.

Socialism is not only a brain disease, but a vast illusion founded upon ignorance and superstition. What Christianity has failed to accomplish socialism now attempts. Socialists in general want to establish the greatest of all dreams, the "Brotherhood of Man," never realizing that no two human beings are ever born alike. Formerly we were told to pray, pray, pray, and now we are told to vote, vote, vote, and I will deliver you from your misery.

Such piffle as "vote for me" may sound beautiful to underdeveloped organisms, but it will never sound good to anyone who reasons. The conscious ego masters himself because he makes and controls his own conditions and environments. Cheap organisms always obey and go to work.

Socialists say the workers must rule industry, but, as they are unable to guide their own destiny, to me it seems impossible for them to control anything outside of themselves.

—W. J. Schilling.

Children a Luxury

The Day Book 28 January 1916.

After reading Kibbler's letter in The Forum I decided to hear the much-talked about Sirfessor Wilkesbarre. And, having heard him, I must say I agree with him inasmuch as he says women are as a general rule the cheaper organism. Why are they? Well, women are not satisfied with breeding "cannon fodder;" they must breed their own competitors in the business world. It is not an unusual sight to see the mother and one or two daughters, sometimes a son, working side by side in a sweatshop. Why do women persist in teaching their sons a false patriotism?

The son of a workingman does not own enough of his so-called country if it was turned into calico to make a canary bird a tea jacket. And if some of the mothers could see their daughters as I have seen them limping around with bunions half the size of a teacup and their toes full of corns from working long hours in the factories and dep't stores (and not only their feet almost killing them but their whole nervous system wrecked), why they would not, they could not oppose birth control.

I am thankful that I am a woman who can say I have never bore any cannon fodder or sweatshop slaves. And I love children better than I love anything in this world. I would love to be surrounded with dozens of them, but they are a luxury I cannot afford.

So, again, I say, I agree with Sirfessor Wilkesbarre. He spoke the naked truth. And that is something the majority of the working class of women do not like to hear.

—Mrs. W. J. Lewis, 1730 Michigan Ave.

Sirfessor Replies

The Day Book 28 January 1916.

I have just finished reading the outpourings of an outraged simpoleon of the name of W. Kibbler, in the Public Forum.

I shall be glad to see Mr. Kibbler, or any other gladiator of socialism, or professional sobbist, refute my postulations which he quotes with such righteous indignation. I am prepared to uphold my position against all comers. Let Mr. K. bring forth his champion of socialism, and let this masterpiece of matter attempt to break the lance of logic on my head on this pregnant proposition: "Exploitation is the first law of individual and industrial progress." That will keep Mr. K. busy thinking until he finds himself out—and in.

Any ego (individual) who does not know that self-realization is the first law of Nature, and that self-preservation is the second law of human Nature, knows as much about the psychology of the soul of man as a pig knows about the perfumes of paradise.

Permit me to say that my name is not Professor Wilkesbarre, but Sirfessor Wilkesbarre.

I am entitled to this term according to the rules of the Society of Superites of England. I do not claim the title "professor."

Re-definitions: an ego is an entity, an individual, and the sum total of all the impigements that register themselves on the grey matter that lies underneath the sinciput, which makes the mind of man.

A simpoleon is a cheap organism, burdened with bifurcated opinions, hard-boiled beliefs and underdone conceptions. He is a purblind proletarian, with parboiled prejudices, putrid principles which he keeps in pickle and hypothetical nebulosities.

—Sirfessor Wilkesbarre

Sirfessor Wilkesbarre

The Day Book 4 February 1916.

Within the last week or so I have been reading a number of letters by individuals who have been attending lectures delivered by Sirfessor Wilkesbarre, and what I have read has impelled me to write these few lines. One of the letters written by W. Kibbler leads me to believe that he holds a deep resentment against the lecturer because he attacks socialism. Another, W. J. Shilling, although he agrees with the lecturer, has sadly misquoted him.

Under these circumstances, and knowing *The Day Book* likes the truth, first hand, I feel it my duty to speak out and tell what I know.

I know and have known Sirfessor Wilkesbarre for many years. He is a very conspicuous figure in England, especially in the North. He is known there as the "Laughing Philosopher of Lancashire."

He has met, to my knowledge, on the public platform some of the finest intellectuals in England. In debate he is invincible, being the most pugnastic and uncompromising debater I have ever heard, and I have heard them all worth while.

In my estimation he can wipe the floor with any man in this country. This is a broad assertion, I admit, but I am saying this with full knowledge of his ability.

His logic is sound and his attitude to the workers seems hostile, but I know long ago he gave up the idea of appealing to them with reason, and so with stinging, biting remarks he whips them into a realization of their pitiful condition, shames them into action, and his work has been effective.

As one of the workers in Manchester, England, a few years ago, when the cause seemed lost and everything seemed black, it was the "Laughing Philosopher of Lancashire," Sirfessor Wilkesbarre, who came along. With bitter words and laughing scorn, he whipped the dying spirits of us workers into action, and we carried everything before us, although others got the credit.

I read with interest of the noble stand of the Welsh miners a few months ago and his, Wilkesbarre's, sudden appearance in that country. Is there any relation between the two I wonder.

Like Thomas Paine he rips the mask of sham and pretense from the hypocrites and fakers and will be appreciated about 100 years after he is dead.

—Our Bill

Definitions

The Day Book 5 February 1916.

Reading the two attacks against the Sirfessor and also hearing the Sirfessor Wilkesbarre, the Messiah of Malfew Seklew, new philosophy of the great ego and his own, on the seven avenues of life, I must comment on this new cult.

I have attended three of his majesty's revivals and heard the satire and sarcasm with which the poor working class are publicly denounced, especially those that are Christians or socialists and stand for democracy. The titles that are bestowed upon the masses are as follows: Simpoleon, living on sympathy; Hopolion, living on hope; Superite, full developed master of the ego; undeveloped organism, a cheap organism; conscious ego, one that is a power over force and matter; an unconscious ego, one living in space and not grounded on matter; socialist, a dreamy simpoleon wallowing and groping at something, never arriving anywhere, but a jaw-smith; Christian, one that has a clotted brain and is a painful sufferer from chronic brain storms, cowardice and divine intoxication. Also the great Sirfessor denounces all form of democracy. His remedy is greased lightning, conscious egos that by minds highly trained will make empires crumble, republics vanish and the world and its wealth will become the property of the superites or conscious egos and the cheap organisms and simpoleons will disappear in fertilizer.

Strange to say, there have been students and scholars attending these intellectual outbursts. The Sirfessor is sure a find and is indeed a public flow of gall and nerve, and as a student I see no need of him calling himself Sirfessor, as that title belongs to a past master of science and not a public ridiculer and slammer at those wishing to know the truth.

—Redwood Bailey[214] (Cherokee Indian).

---

214   "Redwood" Bailey, the famous American Indian, was arrested some time ago for a "seditious"

Socialism Wrong

The Day Book 9 February 1916.

Some of the big and would-be employers do study socialism. Having studied this impossible theory and having seen that it is full of delusions they have handed it down to the honest working class through certain colleges and churches and by various other means.

Government by the people is another illusion and is accepted only those who cannot see any further than the end of their nose. No government rules with the consent of the majority, but in spite of them. The only enemies the workers have may be found among themselves.

Majority votes are certainly a good thing for professional office seekers, but to my mind will never do for the workers. The sooner the worker will think for himself and not for others, and then allow his intellectual capacities to be vivisected by such a modern intellectual as Sirfessor Wilkesbarre—the swiftest microbe that ever landed on American soil—then, and only then, will he be on the road to construction.

—N. J. Schilling, 1244 S. Wabash Ave.

speech made to a street crowd. The "cop" taking him in charge said: "If you don't like this country, why don't you go back to where you came from?'" —*The Seaman's Journal* Volume XXXIII Number 50 (August 18, 1920).

Simple Words from Sirfessor
The Day Book 10 February 1916.

The chaotic emanation from the brain pan of the Cherokee Indian is amusing and confusing. In these days of confusion of thought and fusion of interests it is good for one to stop awhile at the "Temple of Thought" and soliloquise on the frailties, follies, foibles and frenzied fancies of freaks, fakirs, fraudulent formalists and wild-eyes, harem-scarem Reformaniacs.

Malfew Seklew, than whom no swifter mortal ever murdered misery and manufactured mirth, wittily observes in an English paper:

"It's a ghastly sight, a sickly scene,
To see skimmed milk masquerade as cream."

This noble son of the soil has whiskers on his wisdom and is still a Simpoleon. He is only on the threshold of thought. He must mentally digest the "seven wonders of the ego," or "the seven blunders of man," if he desires to escape from defective information, despair, decadency and an early death. If he wants to be born again from the crown downwards, instead of from the feet upwards, send along to me to join my class on the "Evolution of the Ego," and I will teach him the right way to economic power and mental majesty, without money and without price. After he has taken this course I will send him back to the reservation to teach his brother redman the value of reason, revaluation, regeneration and rebellion. He must take this course at his own risk. If he is afraid of battling with new sensations that will make the mentions of his brain spit blood with excitement when a new idea strikes them, then back to mother or the "movement" he must go, still a member of the "Great Unhatched." If he survive the ordeal, he can join the class of Hopeoleons, then join the Sapoleons, afterwards the Social Aristocrats and Conscious Egoists, then onward and upwards towards the Superite, who are walking toward the Superman.

May the blessing of Malfew Skelew rest upon the head of "Our Bill" (see former issue). He is evidently one of the few Egos in USA who has found me out—as I am—a real Messiah of the M(asses) and a Brutalitarian Critic of the Classes.

—Sirfessor Wilkesbarre.

Sirfessor's Satire

The Day Book 11 February 1916.

Do not take Sirfessor Wilkesbarre too seriously. His egoism and superman are only satires and, as such, will start people to think, if nothing else.

There is another side to him. No doubt he is angling for a meal ticket, and, if he can sell a course to develop the superman at a nominal price by following instructions, we can all develop into John Dees or Edisons, why should a course critic object. The only weakness I see in the Sirfessor's argument is that he has not become a superman himself. Perhaps he will enlighten the cheap organisms.

—R. H. Sloan.

These Propositions

The Day Book 11 February 1916.

The propositions of Sirfessor Superite Wilkesbarre:

1. Exploitation is the first law of progress. 2. Socialism is a brain disease. 3. The conscious ego.

No. 1 is right. "Exploit: to the get the value out of anything"—Mr. Webster's *Dictionary*. Capitalism can't distribute what it produces. As an agency of exploitation it must fail. Capitalism cannot utilize the labor-power of society. As an agency of exploitation, again, it must fail.

No. 2 is right: Capitalism is a frenzy. Socialism is a reflection in thought upon the aberrations of capitalism in fact. It shows the cause and cure. It is a brain dis-ease. Also a muscle dis-ease.

No. 3 is right. "Ego," in Latin, means "I." Conscious ego: "You can't fool me." I say: "You can't fool me, either."

It is only when we see two conscious egos with opposite interest that we begin to get an idea of the classification of conscious egos. The one, doing the work of the boss conscious ego, well protected, lords it over the conscious ego who, because his ancestors left him nothing but the world, has to peddle his labor to exist and sheds crocodile tears over the statements of capitalistic apologist who call him "a cheap organism," "a simpoleon" and his ideas "nebulosities."

Some conscious egos, who, being well fed, yet realizing that something is rotten, do not express their material interests in such drastic language, but in "sweeter reasonableness" temper the wind to the shorn lamb by advocating free milk for babies.

And now let me offer a proposition for him to launch his brickbats of solid concrete against: Socialism demands the right to work.

—Double X.

No Quibbler

The Day Book 12 February 1916.

On Feb. 1 I posted a letter to *The Day Book*. It contained my reply to Sirfessor Wilkesbarre and his satellite. Up-to-date it has not appeared in The Forum.

I can think of but two reasons, namely: you did not receive said letter, or you rejected it.

The first reason is a million-to-one shot.

The second needs consideration.

When you reject a letter you usually announce the fact, but not in this case.

I know the Sirfessor is a great man but I did not know *The Day Book* considers him above criticism, especially when he takes such pleasure in criticizing others.

But I think I know the reason, so you will please correct me if I am wrong. So here it is.

Last Sunday I went to the Masonic Temple to hear the Sirfessor once again. When I arrived there I was informed that he would speak at the Colonial Hall, so there I went.

Upon entering I was very much struck by the intelligent-looking individual who pried me loose from the 10 cents admission fee. After I had seated myself I looked around and was astonished to find I had stumbled upon a nest of Public Forum letter writers.

Yes, there, without a doubt, was Mr. Kendrick, accompanied by two bewitching females. And who is that bearded man watching them so intensely? Methinks he kissed two damsels last New Year. Redwood Bailey, the Cherokee Indian, was there with bells on; also a certain condition merchant who makes and controls his own conditions, per order.

Superites were coming and going, bringing chairs to accommodate the enormous crowd. Suddenly a thunderous applause arose and there stood the Sirfessor in all his glory. I looked around for Jesus H. Christ, but I looked in vain.

After the lecture Mr. Block arose and tried to combat the Great Sirfessor, but he met with a crushing defeat. Altogether it was a great success and I came away a sadder but wiser man. Perhaps Mr. Editor, you were kind to me and did not want me to bite off more than I could swallow.

—W. K.

Answers "Just a Girl"
The Day Book 14 February 1916.

You got it right, honey. Most of the guys that write for The Forum are old ginks. The reason Youth and Beauty don't break oftener, as you have noted, is because my articles are usually too long, and sometimes I treat on that great topic which interests you and me (you know) in such fashion that it singes the editor's whiskers and burns the waste basket.

I agree that science and art are ridiculous. If you want to see the real thing come to Sirfessor Wilkesbarre's lectures at Colonial Hall any Sunday at 8. Gee whiz, but that Cranium College is rich! All the Gnuts in town are there, including Allen Steven and myself. (Wait till I get a chew.) Where was I? Oh, yes, I was going to say, what's the matter with introducing something good into the Forum, some real life. You discuss Robert Chambers' heroines and I'll write of the batting averages of the Cubs and Sox. That's a go! Or, better still, let's talk about the weather. It's such good form, you know.

Them there wise guys make me weary. Ho, hum! I guess I'll burn my algebra and bacteriological books and charts and go out and play "Kelly" until I'm broke or somebody else is: either that or I'll get on the phone and call up—never mind. If I land, life will be worth living for a while. Do you get me, "Just a Girl?" Possibly you do.

—John F. Kendrick[215].

---

215   John F. Kendrick was a Chicago-area journalist and IWW supporter. Author of "Christians at War" which begins: Onward Christian soldiers. Duty's way is plain; / Slay your Christian neighbors, or by them be slain, / Pulpiteers are spouting effervescent swill, / God above is calling you to rob and rape and kill." This song appears in *The Little Red Song Book* (1909).

Preparedness

The Day Book 15 February 1916.

Socialism is a goal, distant but worth striving for. Its aim is to secure to the workers of the world the full value of the product of their labor through collective ownership of all industries and Natural resources. The best test of the sincerity of its advocates is afforded by the conduct of those elected to office to carry into effect its principles.

Single Tax is a panacea of the capitalist. Rather than divide their booty with the landlords, the employers of labor desire to hog it all by taxing the land-owner out of business, so that there will be no interference with their profits. In either crass the laborer gets it where he always has gotten it—in the neck.

Religion has been the greatest enemy of progress in the history of mankind. Science has made no discoveries or inventions accepted as matter-of-fact today that have not been bitterly fought by the church because they endangered the belief in a God. More people have been killed in the name of religion than from any other cause. Even in this terrible conflict in Europe the soldiers are spurred on by the belief that "God is on their side."

The mistake of the Sirfessor is in believing that what holds true of the lower animals holds true of man. "Exploitation is the first law of progress" is true of the world that does not reason, but the glory of man is that he is able to improve upon Nature. If this were not so we would have no civilization and no culture. We are trying to make the world better, not worse; to dominate our brutal instincts, not to find the first pretext of yielding to them. The ability of the intellect to property direct our lower instincts distinguishes us from the rest of the Natural world, Sirfessor.

The difference between the idealist and the average man or woman is that the former has a vision and works to realize it, while the latter can see no further than his or her immediate interests, can not one make the most out of life and still see that conditions are wrong and strive to remedy them? I have little doubt that the most persistent chronic kickers in *The Day Book* are the cheeriest optimists at heart. It is their great love for humanity that inspires them to protest feelingly against injustices.

Free love may work out and has worked out successfully in extreme individual cases, but the interest of society would be subserved by perpetuating monogamy. Few women are able to stand alone, and the burden under free love would fall upon the sex least able to bear it.

Preparedness for war spells disaster. The reason we neither got into the European war nor invaded Mexico is because we didn't have the army and navy to fight. Excuses were plentiful. If we prepare to any extent we will have to go to the limit, and with a large army and navy it will be easy to pick any excuse for warfare, even to follow Wilson's idea of protecting abstract justice in any quarter of the globe. That was the idea of the Germans, to civilize the rest of the world. Haven't we got enough to do right here at home? Fight preparedness to the last ditch.

—Thomas Levish[216]

216   Thomas Levish earned 784 votes in the Nonpartisan Aldermanic Elections of Chicago for February 24, 1920. Granted a trade-mark for *Monthly Magazine* on December 12, 1922.

Hard Words

The Day Book 16 February 1916.

Comes one Sirfessor, adumbration of Nietzsche. With linguistic bombast he would impress us, with incoherent verbosity he would confuse us and by vociferous pulmination he would abuse us. He succeed in neither. The verbal contortions and fantastic peregyrations of this grotesque conglomeration of connoted assiduity serves only to amuse.

A more inchoate integration of homogeneous chaos, unconscionable malirudition, inconsistent mental dissipation, undifferentiated intellectual debauchery and misdirected egoistic autointoxication were hard to find. But as one is enough, let us be content to suffer the demented lingual effusions, the hyper-syncopated oratory, the platitudinous labial exudations and the nondescript cerebral phantasmagoria of Wilkesbarre, the miniature Nietzsche.

The manic Nietzsche finds reflex in the Sirfessor's misinform cerebrum, conglomerated from the degenerate serum of diseased royalty, coagulation by a too-indulgent self-communion and aborted by mental dissipation.

Those "Simpoleons" who wish to "get a line" on this "Simpolissimus" may get a volume of Nietzsche, any one will do, open it to any page and read three paragraphs. If perchance the book be held upside down, read anyway. There's just as much logic one way as another. After having read, repeat the magic word Sirfessor and you have Wilkesbarre in replica. Duplicate this process and you have any one of his successful (?) pupils.

Monstrous pomposity contaminated with nauseating insolence and disgusting self-praise is the composite of his intellectual hierarchy and revolting homophobea allied with linguistic monomania in his accoutrement.

The multiform ganglionic gyrations of this neurogymnast with his sclerotic versatility and unrestrained self-adulation should be sufficient to sate the lust of the most dissipated intellectual debauch.

—M. R. Preston.

PS: However much I differ with the Sirfessor, I do not in any way approve the suppression of speech lately put upon him.

Coined Words
The Day Book 16 February 1916.

As I read such nonsense as is contained under the heading: "Simple Words from Sirfessor," I have become convinced that I must enter my protest.

Whatever is meant by "Sirfessor" I don't know, as I have been unable to find same in dictionary. It must be a word invented for the sole purpose of making the average worker believe that he is very low when civilization is considered. I have not been able to define such words as hopoleon, simpoleon, sapoleon, superlite and superman. Why not use common, everyday language, so that all may understand?

Who is this great Malfew Seklew? How true it is that skimmed milk goes around masquerading as cream?

The hope of the workers lies in themselves. If they would vote for their class, which means voting for the Socialist Party and joining the union of their trade, their ambition would be realized. The workers have seen enough of capitalist misrule and now we want the workers to rule themselves.

—J. S.

Panic

The Day Book 17 February 1916.

There is wild panic in the ranks of the "near educated" in Chicago owing to the sudden appearance in our midsts of Sirfessor Wilkesbarre, the Laughing Philosopher of Lancashire. His fame has gone before him, and now we have the ghastly sight and sickly scenes of seeing all the skimmed milk masquerading as cream hunting for cover.

One of our public lecturers, Mr. Percy Ward, who was a member of the Bradlaugh Debating Club of Bradford, England, at the same time as the Sirfessor, informed the others what to expect and consequently we lookers-on are amused at this wild scramble of the "elite."

Like the orthodox preacher of old our present professional sobist and yearnist will take advantage of every excuse—morality, vulgarity, brutality—anything and everything rather than come out of their holes and meet this "grim old warrior" on the public platform.

The Sirfessor's hat is in the ring with a challenge to all, bar none. His fame is spreading, his supporters are growing more numerous and sooner or later our present "denouncers of the system" will be smoked out of their holes and then the fun will begin.

In the mean time, we who earnestly desire the truth will do all in our power to bring this thing about as soon as possible and dash into the future regardless of the past.

So I say: Here's to Sirfesor Wilkesbarre, may he go on with the good work he has so well begun. For as Malfew Seklew once said: "The Molecule of Mirth has set out to reconnoiter, to murder the Microbe of Misery, and the Election of Ecstasy has set out to assist in the assassination of the Atom of Agony."

—Our Bill.

Altruism

The Day Book 19 February 1916.

Amidst cheering and applause by an enthusiastic audience, *The Gospel According to Malfew Seklew* received another boost in the form of a lecture delivered by Sirfessor Wilkesbarre.

The subject under discussion was "Altruism." This destructive disease was clearly defined and vivisected by the greatest humorist and brutalitarian truthist that ever landed on American soil, who took the pleasure in exposing same.

The Sirfessor proved beyond a shadow of a doubt that the majority of people are suffering from this disease, which is international in scope. Among his remarks it was clearly shown that conscious is a product of altruism. Socialism, Christianity and various other delusions were assailed per order and held responsible for its perpetuations.

Christianity, whose foundation is based upon mythology, was held responsible for introducing this dangerous disease, found guilty of high treason and was condemned as an enemy of the people. The "golden rule" was bitterly attacked and denounced in a way that the entire audience shouted with joy.

Nietzsche, whom many of the intellectual world consider one of the ablest writers that the world has ever produced, says as follows:

> Christianity was a victory; a nobler type of character was destroyed by it.
>
> Christianity has been (and still is) the greatest misfortune of makind.

May the philosophy of Malfew Seklew and Nietzsche be installed in the minds of all.

—W. J. Schilling, 1244 S. Wabash Av.

Stomach Pads

The Day Book 21 February 1916.

I looked upon John Healy's outpouring, in which he accused radicals of deserting their cause as soon as they got their stomachs full, as being merely a reflection of his own mind or his own line of action if he is or if he were to become a radical.

The type he speaks of—and I have no doubt there are some—could not be classed as radicals at all. They are just stomach rebels, who have no ideal other than their own stomachs. Just another case, as Malfew Seklew would say, of skimmed milk masquerading as cream.

—W. Kibbler

Nietzsche

The Day Book 22 February 1916.

I beg leave to explain what Sirfessor Wilkesbarre preaches.

I have had the extreme pleasure of listening to the Sirfessor's lectures and found him to be an excellent expounder and popularizer of Max Stirner's and Nietzsche's philosophy. His mode of popularizing these great men's philosophy is by laughing them out of the philosophy of altruism and into the consciousness of the ego. For, according to Nietzsche, altruism is a slave morality, encouraging self-denial and killing self-reliance, and as he postulates that the "I" is older and stronger than the "Thou," by ridiculing the egos who have been caught in the trap of slavish altruism, he tends to awaken them to their real importance.

Proclaiming the "Thou" and neglecting the "I" leads to the depths of slavery. Altruism is meant for the other fellow, not for oneself.

As soon as the masses realize themselves and become conscious of their power then we will see the glimmer of the dawn of a new day. This new day will be the evolution of man to surpass himself and to become a superman. A superman is a man who will follow this who represent his own thoughts, ideas and principles and will not follow anybody blindly, nor attempt by cunning devices to ensnare others to follow him for his own special benefit and for their enslavement.

In the noble words of Nietzsche:

> Now I bid you lose me and find yourself; and only when you have denied me will I return to thee again.[217]

I believe that such a philosophy is the greatest mental tonic and stimulate real and true clear thinking. It points to no clear

---

217   From *Thus Spoke Zarathustra*.

economic goal, but if men were to become impregnated with such noble thoughts human salvation would be near at hand: for it develops a healthy psychology by urging the individual to believe in himself, and he in turn should urge his fellowmen to do likewise.

—Sam Druck.

Growing

The Day Book 24 February 1916.

I may be skimmed milk, but I am far away from masquerading or trying to make others believe that I am anything more than I am.

Getting to understand something that we could not understand before is not necessarily sneaking out of a hole; neither is it right to call a man a crank who simply tries to teach others what he thinks is right, no matter how ridiculous it may seem to us; for many a man who was considered a crank turned out to be a brainy benefactor. We are all yearning for something to come one way or the other.

I am a thoroughbred evolutionist. I believe that things are just as they were intended to be and that they grow for better or worse according to the change of time.

It is well for a teacher to use simple common sense words and refrain from calling his pupils out-of-the-way names. I can never get to believe that it is right for one to think alone of himself and not a little of others who may not have the power to be an unconscious, self-loving conscious ego.

We may all crawl out of our holes eventually and get to be level-headed people and get to understand that the only way to live right is to live and let live and to build up the world for the good of all peoples and not for the few. I am afraid that the teachings of Malfew Seklew aren't altogether right when it comes to bettering the conditions of all mankind. His doctrine is only good for the ones capable of practicing it and perhaps will take much longer to bring about the real justice than any other way.

—Frank Smith.

Sirfessor's Pedigree

The Day Book 26 February 1916.

I noticed by *The Day Book* that the latest imposition from England is causing quite a sensation. I refer to the well-known President of the Society of Superites, Sirfessor Wilkesbarre. The Society that he is so well representative of has produced many great thinkers. To mention just a few: The famous Lawrence Smith, who is called the Sage of Harpurhey; Toole, the Cherub of Denton; Paley, the Street Car Saint; "Tom Winter," the ex-Roman Catholic Bishop; Mrs. Winter, whose reputation is revered in India, where she is considered as high as any of the religious Mahatmas. Finally, the greatest of all women of Scottish birth, Spencella Maljean.

There are many I am sure who have enjoyed the pleasure of their friendship and who cherish the association for the mental pleasure derived therefrom. And the Sirfessor himself, he need have no fear from those who deny his credentials.

While I disagree with Wilkesbarre himself, I cannot but help admire his wonderful method of presenting a subject. His theories may be "unpopular" to the Socialists and Christians, but if they disagree, at least let them get an opponent to debate the question. There are, however, few in the United States who can successfully combat the position laid down by the greatest of the apostles of Malfew Seklew. For such is the standard of F. M. Wilkesbarre.

—T. T., Winnipeg, Can.

Of Men

The Day Book 26 February 1916.

Although I do not agree with Sirfessor Wilkesbarre in many things, it does not get me anywhere by calling him harsh names. Yet I am forced to admit that in some of his arguments I can find no answer.

For instance, he says: "Democracy is the rule of the majority, and the majority always consists of the ignorant many, consequently the voice of the one who knows is drowned by the mass of matter who do not know."

To me this seems correct. History proves it.

I also think, as Sirfessor Wilkesbarre says: "We are purblind proletarians, with parboiled prejudices and putrid principles which we keep in pickle."

I would have still been in the Moody church if some individual had not come along and dispelled my delusions, which, by the way, I bitterly resented at the time, but after a close investigation of Christianity I found he was right, and as I want the truth I for one intend to hear all sides of the argument and decide for myself.

—W. Kibbler.

Love

The Day Book 4 March 1916.

Love is the expression of the human mind or soul. It's the union of two in one. Love is represented by a factor and a component in man and woman. Love is not the mind, but holds the same relation to the mind that light holds to the eye. It is the light that makes the eye of service to man; so with love. It preserves the mind, so it can be transmitted from one generation to another. Without mind man would be like a blind person groping in the dark, not knowing what he is doing or why he is doing it. In the days of Judaism love was represented by the all-seeing eye. The keystone in the arch of Solomon's temple represented the mind, with the eye in the center. The mind, being material like the eye, takes love to illuminate it and make it useful to man. Don't trifle with love. If you want to see the result of trifling, pay Dunning a visit. Mind produces two senses, knowledge and understanding. *The Day Book* has many advocates of polygamy and plural marriages. They are only the apeings of our college Sirfessor and other mouth organs that try to fool the people.

St. Paul says: "Without love we are nothing."

Our system of economics, religion and education is evidence that we have no learned men among us. We have the ethical and literary, but the learned are few. The Romans played a mean trick on the people in forbidding the priests to marry. The priest have no more mind than a bat, as they sold their birthright to be a priest. He has no love; does not know what love is; consequently he has no mind, as love is the evidence of mind. No person can know what love really is until he is married to a loving wife and has children of his own. Born of love, then he learns what loves is. He is not only willing to work for their keeping, but sacrifice his life in their defense.

It should be the aim of all men to produce the man according to the law and the original plan. The Christian's aim is to reform man. They have plans only, as they are devoid of mind, and they think man is spiritual. They don't know and can't understand God's ways. All manual workers interested in the future welfare of your brothers, don't countenance polygamous or plural marriages.

—E. Sweeney.

Wilkesbarre

The Day Book 9 March 1916.

While speaking with a member of the Society of Social Aristocrats he disclosed the very interesting information, namely: *The Tribune* has refused to accept his advertisements for Sunday meetings. If you will remember a few weeks ago Sirfessor Wilkesbarre, who is President of the Society, was refused a hall in the Masonic Temple. My own observations have told me that he has been chopped out of The Public Forum. Would you please inform me, Mr. Editor, why *The Tribune* and *Day Book* stand together on this? What is wrong with this man that both capitalists and progressive newspapers wish to gag him? I am interested and would like to know. Hoping *The Day Book* will not suppress this letter.

—Wm. Kibbler.

Editor's Note:[218] Nobody has been chopped out of The Public Forum. All contributions look alike to us, and all contributors will be judged by their public interest. Wilkesbarre has no kick coming.

---

218   Above note was the editor of *The Day Book*.

The Gospel According to Malfew Seklew

Kibbler Kids Kend'r'k

The Day Book 11 March 1916.

I have been nursing a complaint against *The Day Book* which I find upon examination to be groundless.

I was much interested in J. Kendrick's proposed group of photographs of Forum writers. I think I would be well able to fulfill the part he has allotted for me. Mr. Kendrick does not say what part he would take in this picture, so I suggest that he and that Beautiful Creature who usually accompanies him to Sirfessor Wilkesbarre's meetings pose as Adam and Eve in the Garden of Eden, naming the animals, with Allan Steven disguised as the serpent in the background, the Sirfessor posing as the Tree of Knowledge and Redwood Bailey with a flaming sword standing at the gate keeping out the rest of the bunch.

—W. Kibbler.

Everybody's Business

The Day Book 11 March 1916.

How is socialism helping the wage slave, Simpoleon or working man? What has been the result for the last 20 years?

What's everybody's business is nobody's business. Before people can do anything to better conditions they must be educated and do it themselves and not leave it to the political parities. You see, socialism is a pure failure. If you would like to argue on this subject meet me at Sirfessor Wilkesbarre's meeting, Colonial Hall.

—Harry Plotkin.

Too Much Ego

The Day Book 8 April 1916.

The Sirfessor is said to have many apt students. His teaching that the will to live is only sufficient for cheap organisms, but dear organisms develop a will to power and are not overly scrupulous as to how they attain it, doesn't work out in practice.

Acting on his teaching a goodly number are said to have run the blockade at the door of the Sirfessor's meetings and listened to the dulcet strains of the Sirfessor's voice and the seven wonders of the ego without contributing coin toward the expenses of the meeting, which shows that the Sirfessor's ego lacks something to make him a superite.

Too much ego is apt to give one the big head. As an individual brick is one of the units in a brick building, so an individual ego is a unit in the collectivity. The strength of the building depends upon all of the bricks. A super brick along with the poor brick makes a poor building. Only where all the bricks are super will we have a super building. So a superman, along with a lot of brains, make a bad society and render the ego of little account when developed. The will to power wants to be tempered with justice and mercy. The ego may be a good thing, fully developed, but we can get too much of a good thing, as the Sirfessor can now testify.

—D. F. Sweetland, 2259 S. Kildare Av.

To Bess H.

The Day Book 10 July 1916.

I am certainly pleased that you take an interest in me. You ask so many questions that I can only answer a few of them. You seem to object because I scold like a parrot at times, but just console yourself that a parrot does not know what it is talking about.

You flatter me with a college professorship. I am sorry to say that I would not last as long as Scott Nearing did at that work, because I would not agree with anybody and they would get sore the same as you did.

I used to work 16 hours a day, 7 days a week but people thought less of me than when I quit and worked only 5 hours, 5 1/2 days a week.

Alimonycally speaking, I am not worth the thought of catching, because the dozen dollars or so I bring home each week for my hard word is not enough to get excited over.

I am just a cheap clerk and a cheap roomer. My room is off from the kitchen because I like to camp as near the food as possible.

Now that you know all this, do you still feel worried about my single condition? If so, why don't you try to convert me to double blessedness? I don't say that you will succeed, but it might relieve your mind.

Sirfessor Wilkesbarre says: "self-exploitation is the first law of progress." Maybe you would be more pleased if I had married and still posed as single.

Come over some time and see me. Bring your friends and servants. You have read how grand my personage is because I have described it repeatedly.

Since you have read so much and are still a "doubting Thomas," come to my house. I will promise you that you will be like the Queen of Sheeba, who visited the court of Solomon. It was so much better than she thought it would be she exclaimed: "the half has never yet been told."

I have no gold to offer, but mental peace, mental happiness and joy. I care not what your trouble may be. With my feet on top of the piano, table or as near the ceiling as I can reach or some other unconventional style, I will await your criticism.

—Allen Steven.

The IWW

The Day Book 5 October 1916.

History has recorded many forms of tyranny by rulers or sets of rulers holding the reigns of power. But I do not know of any form of tyranny more contemptible than practiced by members of the IWW in some of the western sates, where the slogan is: "If you do not carry an IWW card you cannot ride a train." Of course, this applies to the hobo.

A poor, defenseless hobo beating it over a division is easy picking for a gang of organized bums (see hymn 25 of *The Little Red Song Book*), when not being able to show an IWW card he is promptly thrown off the train.

The state of Utah showed its power when it murdered Joe Hillstrong, a despotic act over which the IWW shed crocodiles tears on every other street corner. But I think if they, the IWW, had shown half as much energy and direct action on behalf of Hillstrong as they do in throwing some poor hobo off a train there would have been no funeral in Chicago.

Despotism is despotism, no matter whether coming from the Czar of Russia, the Pope of Rome or the IWW, and being a rebel in the true sense of the word I raise my voice against this particular brand.

As Sirfessor Wilkesbarre says: "give cheap organisms power and they will use it in a cheap way."

—W. Kibbler.

Who Can Answer?

The Day Book 28 October 1916.

There are a great many people in Chicago who would like to have the following questions answered:

Are Ragnar Redbeard, the author of *Might is Right*, and Sirfessor Wilkesbarre one and the same individual?

There is quite a difference of opinion on this question.

Also, will the many followers of Sirfessor Wilkesbarre have the pleasure of hearing Malfew Seklew himself this coming winter?

Knowing that Sirfessor Wilkesbarre is a constant reader and admirer of *The Day Book*, I am sure this letter will be read by him and perhaps he will give me the information I desire.

—W. Kibbler.

Steven is Popular

The Day Book 18 November 1916.

Malfew Seklew once said: "Brave men love danger; that is why they pursueth women." But I do not know what he would say if the situation were reversed, as it was last Sunday night at Sirfessor Wilkesbarre's meeting when no less than five ladies asked the manager whether Allen Steven was present. Upon being answered in the negative five ladies sat in five different parts of the hall and five pairs of eyes watched the entrance.

As Allen Steven is a regular attender his arrival was expected every moment by the manager but strange to say he—Allen Steven—did not appear that night.

After the meeting five disappointed ladies faded away into the atmosphere, each one unconscious of the other one's presence.

There are many wild rumors in circulation regarding Allen Steven by readers of *The Day Book*, but one thing is certain. Namely, that Allen is very popular with the ladies.

—W. Kibbler.

Advice to Allen

The Day Book 24 November 1916.

W. Kibbler's article brings to mind Allen Steven's article in which he related the gymnastic stunts he was doing, thereby injuring his toe, which may be in a sling yet, and he could foreswear one meeting of Sirfessor Wilkesbarre's in preference to losing his toe altogether.

My! What a time these seven wives will have, each one breaking her neck to bandage the toe first. I wonder if the manager knows Allen Steven. I recall a letter in The Forum last winter wherein the contributor referred to Allen as "the bewhiskered gentlemen with that sweet young thing beside him." The manager has another look coming, or else Allen removed his whiskers before presenting himself to me, and, again, when one considers having seven wives to keep and a dog, each one wanting (except the dog) to read *The Day Book* now that it has risen a cent. The wisest thing to do is to sit at home or be content with a nickel show once a week.

Who knows? Those five ladies may have been five of Allen's wives and had one slipped over on them. He may have taken two of the wives to the picture show.

I suggest to Steven to wear a red hatband, by which he may be known, or come walking in on stilts. I hope all concerned will continue reading *The Day Book*. I will, and will watch to see the speedy recovery of Allen's toe. I also give him the timely advice to keep his feet on *terra firma* in the future and not follow the high cost of living.

—A Constant Reader.

He Hit the Nail

The Day Book 24 November 1916.

Sirfessor Wilkesbarre hit the nail on the head last Sunday, judging from the applause, at his meeting held at 20 W. Randolph, when he said *The Day Book* is a unique organ; the only daily paper in Chicago which could be classified as a free press, the only paper in Chicago which announced his meetings. That fact alone made it well worth buying if it cost a dollar per copy. He admired Mr. Cochran for his sagacity, veracity and audacity, and that any of its present readers who did not continue as such were cheap organisms, financially and mentally.

These statements coming form a man who slams everybody and everything were quite refreshing. While the Sirfessor was delivering himself of this outburst, Allen Steven almost threw a fit, and but for the restraining hand of his lady friend would have mounted a chair to demonstrate his approval. I was very pleased to hear this from the Sirfessor, as I have at last found something that mutually agree on.

—W. Kibbler.

How to Stop Murder
The Day Book 25 January 1917.

If everybody will listen to me they will not commit murders, unless they are insane. A man is a cur who will induce a passionate, sexually-strong woman to love him, kiss him—yes, everything, and then cruelly spill her blood in murder.

A guy like that, rich or poor, ought to be burned at the stake; hanging is too good for him. Probably half of the married folks got married because they thought they had to, in order to hide their sins, and I wish the other half had sinned before marriage; then nobody would dare throw mud at our "Magdalenes."

It should be a sort of religious ritual, a betrothal, a trial marriage, indulged in by all before the age of 21. Then there would be no goats in society. It would reduce murders 25 percent, and all mental punishments, suicides, sorrows, etc. would vanish like vapors, because we would all be in the same boat.

Today we have the marriage caste, the singular caste, and one preys on the frailties of the other. It is really a form of mental murder that leads often to actual murder. Society itself is responsible for all this class of murder and this includes all people afflicted with Puritan "Intolerance." The Committee of Fifteen[219] would not admit they are indirect murderers because they are not philosophers.

Harry Thaw[220] killed White in a fit of jealousy, which is an uncalled-for condition of mind. Verily, verily, I say unto you, consider Nat Goodwin: he shoots not, neither does he kill, yet he grants divorces and plasters them all with alimony and

---

219 The Committee of Fifteen lobbied against prostitution and gambling in 1900.
220 Harry Kendall Thaw (1871 - 1947), heir to a multi-million dollar mine and railroad fortune, murdered Stanford White (1853 - 1906), architect, over White's affair with Thaw's wife Florence Evelyn Nesbit (1884 - 1967), subject of the film *The Girl in the Red Velvet Swing* (1955).

comes up smiling. That is the kind of men we should have. He lives and let lives.

A woman kills a husband once in a while. Why? Because divorces are hard to get and she is mismatched. Give her a free divorce when she wants it and she will not murder her husband; neither will she breed dome moron children by this mismatched man, which is the bigger crime. She choses the lesser evil and murders him, thus proving herself to be a real philosopher, and the trial jury has brains enough to see this, but the "public Shylock," the state's attorney, who seeks his "pound of flesh," his conviction, does not want to admit the truth.

Sirfessor Wilkesbarre says that "one of the most ruthless murderers is the meek maiden who goes out into the garden and cruelly pulls out a growing onion from the ground and eats it raw like a cannibal, without even giving it chloroform." But I was only mentioning foolish human murders unnecessary to progress.

—Allen Steven, 3854 N. Robey.

A Divorce Cure

The Day Book 16 February 1917.

Just because I believe in divorce, free and easy to obtain, is not saying that I would urge couples to run off and seek divorce on the slightest provocations.

Life is earnest, real and many times a tragedy at best. A little quarrel, argument or piqued disposition should not necessarily lead to separation. Many times a man or woman is mad, but can't tell what about. A little counsel with wiser and older heads might lead to a lifelong understanding and permanent love.

I think our divorce judges aim to be fair to all concerned. Judge Stelke's plans of a friendly little talk I think grand. There is a test or two I would like the judge to try first on the man, then another for the woman.

Suppose we take wifey, who wants a divorce from hubby, to a banquet so that she may see and hear other men in action. Suppose we sit her down to a table full of such fellows as Sirfessor Wilkesbarre, Lochman, Jack Carney, Geo. V. Wells, Sweetland, Jesus Christ of South Halsted St., myself and similar deluded nuts. Let her listen to the toasts and after dinner talks of these fellows and then decide for herself whether her John is any worse.

Suppose the Sirfessor would start off: "You are all cheap organisms and I am the real superman. You are all masses of matter that don't matter, pestiferous pifflers with warts on your imaginations, and if you had the brains of a jellyfish or a soft-boiled egg you would all wake up and be conscious egos."

Suppose after she listened to this "outburst of agony" she next heard our old friend Lochman, who might say: "Pay no attention to this half-baked nut who is kidding himself into believing he is a superite, when in fact the only place he exercises super qualities is in 'One Arm' Thompsons's restaurant with a poor, helpless cheese sandwich and a cup of coffee. Now remember, friends, the only time you are lucky is when you are dead."

Suppose next she heard Sweetland tell how a man lost the right to vote years ago because his mule died, the vote based on property the man had. Suppose Sweetland ended it all by exclaiming: "Oh, I forgot! I spoke from these same notes a week ago."

I believe after the woman wanting divorce heard all us fellows she would stretch out her arms to heaven and exclaim: "My poor, dear hubby with all his faults is worth a whole barnyard full of superites, cheap organisms, half-baked nuts, absent-minded rebels, second deluded Christs and Mormons he saved me from when he married me. Me back to John and no divorce."

—Allen Steven, 3854 N. Robey.

BELLOWS and RECOLLECTIONS

The Eagle and The Serpent

A Journal for Free Spirits and for Spirits struggling to be Free.

The proudest animal under the sun and the wisest animal under the sun have set out to reconnoitre.

Edited by JOHN ERWIN McCALL.

Associate Editor, MALFEW SEKLEW.

Vol 2. No. 5. SEPTEMBER, 1902. PRICE 1/- (25 CENTS).

Principal Contents:

PUBLISHED TO THE TRADE BY

WATTS & CO., 17, Johnson's Court, Fleet Street, London, E.C.

Subscription & Editorial Address:

26 *Clovelly Mansions, Gray's Inn Road, London, W.C., England.*

NEXT ISSUE (A THOREAU NUMBER) READY JANUARY FIRST.

Cover of The Eagle and The Serpent, *published September, 1902, containing the essay "Egoism: Conscious and Unconscious."*

J. Bruce Glasier: Demi-Gods Demi-Damned, or Halo's Hoodooed

Bradford: J. W. Gott 1909.

"We may say at once we have no patience with such intellectual poltroons."
—New Age.

"The truest jests sound worse in guilty ears."[221]

"To know the disease is half the cure."[222]

"I hate, where I looked for a manly forbearance, or at least a manly resistance, to find a mush of concession. Better to be a nettle in the side of a friend than his echo."[223]
—Emerson.

"You are trying to carry on an heroic policy without using any heroism. You nourish the absurd aspiration that you can do good without doing any harm—can help justice without hurting injustice. Your Love Campaign is sublimely ineffectual."[224]
—Prof. Barnhill.

"Brethren, we must become more bitter. Bitterness is the best antidote to the Christian slave-pox which for two thousand years has poisoned our blood."[225]
—Prof. Barnhill.

"The doctrine of hatred must be preached as the counteraction to the doctrine of love when that pules and whines."[226]
—Emerson.

"Nothing will be done till Hate is in the saddle—till we have a race which hates rent, hates robbery."[227]
—John Erwin McCall.

221   Quote appears in *The College Irish Grammar* by Ulick Joseph Bourke (1856).
222   Miguel de Cervantes Saavedra (1547 - 1616). Author. Quote from *Don Quixote de la Mancha, Book 2*.
223   Ralph Waldo Emerson (1803 - 1882). Author. Quote from *Essays: First Series* (1841). Quote also appears in *The Eagle and The Serpent* Volume 2 Number 5 (September 1902).
224   *The Eagle and the Serpent* Volume 2 Number 5 (September 1902).
225   *Ibid.*
226   Quote from *Essays: First Series* (1841). Quote also appears in *The Eagle and The Serpent* Volume 2 Number 5 (September 1902).
227   *The Eagle and The Serpent* Volume 2 Number 5 (September 1902).

"There are no poor such as God hates."

"How few think of the thinking few,
How many never think who think they do."[228]

"It is the fools who do the work of the world, and the wise
who profit by it."[229]

J. Bruce Glasier[230], the blue-eyed He-Belle of State Socialism and
Democratic "Cock o' the North," left his country for the good of his
health, and to escape his early environment. He arrived in "Merrie
England" with good intentions, his indentures, vaccination marks in
good condition, and his soul saturated with the Syrup of Sympathy.

After a severe struggle in the University of Adversity, he
achieved success as a Professer of Piffle to the "Great Unhatched,"
and made his mark among the Miss-Messiahs of the Masses as
an eloquent exponent of the Mass-Mind.

He parts his name in the middle, as is the fashion among
the "aristocrats" of Labor—J. Keir Hardie[231], J. Ramsay Mac-
Donald[232], H. Russell Smart[233], T. Gavan-Duffy[234], etc., etc.

In the nights of his Nonage he was a romping, roaring, revolutionary Anarchist and earnest Atheist; now he is a Defender
of Mrs. Grundy and the Sermon on the Mount (a sermon for
slaves), and an enemy of "God and my neighbor."

A mournful melodist in kilts and a star-gazing Idealist, afflicted with inflammation of the Imagination, he mistakes perspiration for inspiration.

"The Blight of Respectability" overpowers him, and renders
him powerless to progress beyond his prejudices, for he is a person of great principles which he preserves in pickle till they be-

228   Quote attributed to "An Ex-M.A." in *Notes and Queries* (February 27 1869) and later (1885) to
"Alektor" in the same journal.
229   Quote attributed to Josh Wise in the New Zealand newspaper *Marlborough Express*, Volume
XLIII Number 168 (July 14 1909).
230   John Bruce Glasier (1859 - 1920). Socialist.
231   James Keir Hardie (1856 - 1915). Socialist.
232   James Ramsay MacDonald (1866 - 1937). Prime Minister.
233   H. Russell Smart. Author of *Socialism and Drink* (1890).
234   Rev. T. Gavan Duffy (1888 - 1942). Missionary.

come great prejudices.

He parades his principles—when they are not prejudices—to suit his opportunity. He is an unscrupulous Moralist, a Jesuitical, Political Policy Pusher, and Special Pleader for the "Academy of Altruists, and Moral Debauchees and Emotional Acrobats," who manipulate the minds and monies of the members of the Independent Labour Party.

He is the Pope of the Editorial room of the *Labor Leader*, when the "devil" is away.

Autocrat of the literature tables of the I.L.P., he has put upon the *Index Expurgatorius*[235] the publications of the R.P.A. and has kicked under the table "The Bottom Dog" of Robert Blatchford[236]—the Manufacturer of the Socialist Movement in England. For there is no malice like the malice of the moralist and virtues can be just as dangerous as vices—and more so—if put to improper use. Perhaps he knows not "that the Devil divides the world between Atheism and Superstition." He aspires to be the Brutus of the Body Politic and the Savior of the Body Social, but he knows as much about the "Missing Link" of Economics as the *Pithecanthropus Erectus*[237] knows about the "Soul of Man under Socialism,"[238] or as much about the Spirit of Freedom as the Microbe of Misery knows of the "Music of the Spheres."

He is an Ex-Knight of Labor inundated with a craving to be the Prophet of Political Socialism, and professional "Spellbinder," re the Rights of Man[239] and the Wrongs of Woman[240].

He is a tamed element in the shape of a man since he got his marriage lines and became the lawfully-wedded husband of Katherine B. St. John Conway, J. Bruce Glasier, B.A.(H.)[241] and an en-

---

235   The Index Expurgatorius is the periodic update to The *Index Librorum Prohibitorum*, the list of forbidden books published by the Roman Catholic Church.
236   Robert Peel Glanville Blatchford (1851 - 1943). Atheist. Author of *Not Guilty: A Defence of the Bottom Dog* (1905).
237   *Pithecanthropus Erectus* aka *Homo erectus erectus* was discoverd in 1891.
238   Oscar Fingal O'Flahertie Wills Wilde (1854 - 1900). Author of *The Soul of Man under Socialism* (1891).
239   *Rights of Man* (1791) a book by Thomas Paine (1737 - 1809).
240   *Maria: Or, The Wrongs of Woman* (1798), posthumous book by Mary Wollstonecraft (1759 - 1797).
241   Katharine Glasier (1867 - 1950) and John Bruce Glasier (1859 - 1920). Socialists.

thusiastic Evangelist of the Religion of Sorrow and Degeneration.

He is so moral that he carries his marriage lines with him to preserve his reputation and to appease the wrath of Mrs. Grundy and the Mrs.

He repudiates Free Love, advocates marriage as it is regardless of the fact that marriage is the only trade which every woman can work at—as a slave without a wage. He prefers Free Luncheons for the children to Free Thought among Reformers.

He exhibits the Divinity of Hate only when he denounces the capitalist system—which he hates with a feeble-forcibleness—the while he advocates the Brotherhood of man and the Gospel of Faith. He uses the lash of love to lacerate the hearts of men and produce hysterical agitations in the bosoms of women.

When the heart is afire some sparks will fly out at the mouth, especially when one knows that the pleasures of the mighty are the tears of the poor; and also that "Society is based upon the patience of the poor." This is enough to make an amiable freak take to drink—or decapitate a hard-boiled egg in his agony. He is not brutal enough to be Great; for he speaks with a tear-drop in one eye—and a look of scorn in the other as he vomits forth soft arguments wrapped in the hard words, in the endeavor to plant a Heaven in the midst of this Hell on Earth.

Heine says, "Christianity is the sickness period of Humanity."[242] It seems to me that Bruce Glasier, wife and other intellectual invalids, represent "the sickness period of Socialism." Without a guide they will never find the Right Road to the Millennium, because "There's no seeing one's way through tears."[243]

In the Cave of Adullam[244] I leave this *soi-disant* Damon of Democracy, sitting serene and satisfied with his "outlook"— and his situation as the Shah of the Sentimentalists. His motto is *"Dum spero, spiro."*[245]

242   Christian Johann Heinrich Heine (1797 - 1856). Author. Quote from *The Memoirs of Mister von Schnabelewopski* (1834).
243   British proverb.
244   The Cave (or Fortress) of Adullam is mentioned in 1 Samuel 22:1.
245   *Dum spiro spero* translates to "While I breathe, I hope." Malfew Seklew presumably here

"POLITICS AND PARLIAMENT."

"Behold, my son, with how little wisdom the world is governed."

—John Belden.

"Rich men without conviction are more dangerous in modern society than poor women without chastity."

—G. B. Shaw.

"The House of Lords—An institution at which the divorced meet the divines to resist the destitute."

—*Truth*.

"The House of Commons—An institution at which the representatives of the people sell the interests of the constituents."

—*Truth*.

"The Englishman is never so happy as when he is ostentatiously reforming—something, so long as it is not himself."[246]

Polities is the Battle of the Ballot. It Is a Battle for a Bauble. The Electors play with the Bauble while the "Elected" juggle with the "Boodle." The ballot is the battle-cry of bipeds looking for peace, retrenchment and reform, for they think it is the Bulwark of "John Bull and his Island," the Palladium of their liberties, and the Pass-key to Progress. It was given to the common people—after much agitation—by Disraeli, the wisest Jew, and wittiest, and wickedest Statesman of the 19th Century, because I believe he saw that it would soothe the Republican soothsayers into quietude—as it certainly has done, for there are no Red Republicans to be found nowadays in England.

---

suggests the opposite.

246   Quote from an article printed in *The Nation*, December 14th, 1905.

Another thing that few reformers know is, that as the franchise has been extended, the powers of the police have been enlarged, until today we have practically a police army, commanded by military officers, who are rapidly Germanising and Russianising the system. At the present time the police tyrannise over the shopkeepers until they are in a state of mental meekness; and terrorise the lower orders of society until they drive the strong into jail, and the weak into silent slavery and dumb submission.

The people prefer the arbitrament of the ballot to the arbitrament of the bullet, forgetful of the fact that Liberty will never be granted, but must be taken. The arbitrament or the ballot is a renunciation of arbitration: a glorification of the rule of the majority; with its corollary the enslavement and subjection of the minority. It is the rule of Force—not the reign of Equality, Fraternity, and Liberty, which so many yearn for.

The ballot is not a panacea for the ills of society, nor a nepenthe for the sorrows of the common people, but a pseudo-paraclete that fills the calamity-howler with beatific bliss, minds thought: a mental hasheesh that holds the helot in leash without the lash; and transforms the Revolutionist into an Evolutionist saturated with optimism, and delirious day dreams.

Politics is a game played in Parliament. It is a pastime for the idle rich, and a game of bluff, mixed with blarney and bunkum for the poor. It is a confidence game played upon the people, for the people are persuaded into the belief that Parliament respects the Will of the People. While the truth is Parliament is actually an instrument to preserve the privileges of the rich, and to strengthen their position, founded on economic power. Parliament really registers the power of the owners of economic wealth in the shape of land, money, and other kinds of property. Property rules the Rostrum of Parliament, as surely as self-interest rules the world.

"The People is a beast of muddy brain
That knows not its own force, and therefore stands
Loaded with wood and stone: the powerless hands
Of a mere child guide it with bit and rein:
But the beast fears, and what the child demands,
It does; nor Its own terror understands,
Confused and stupified by bugbears vain,
Most wonderful! With its own hand it ties
And gags itself—gives itself death and war.
For peace doled out by Kings from its own store,
Its own are all things between earth and heaven;
But this it knows not: and if one arise
To tell the truth, it kills him unforgiven."[247]

They know not that Might is Right and Justice is built on property qualifications.

Political power is the recognition of class interests. All political reform is the outcome of class agitation to cement class interests. Economic power always precedes political privileges. Politics is an appanage, and an appendage of property. Politics prove the power of policy over principle. The power of principle is the principal part of progress. As Hazlitt has it: "Great acts grow out of great principles, working changes in Society, and tearing it up by the roots."

The prejudices of the Picaroon appear to dominate the actions and ambitions of the professional politician, rather than the principles of the purist.

The proof of principle is honesty of purpose. Politics—as given to the poor but honest workingman—consist mainly of piffle, platitudes, and programmes without principle. "Honesty is the best policy," so the moralists murmur. It may be the best principle, but it has ever been the worst policy—in the politics of today, yesterday, and doubtless will be the same in the politics of tomorrow. Politics is the Might of the Mouth over Righteousness of Thought. The great secret for the people to

---

247 *The People* by Tommaso Campanella, Italian philosopher, 1568–1639. Translation by John Addington Symonds.

understand is that the owners of the economic foundations of Society are manufacturers of the religion, morality, politics, law and justice that prevail in the locality in which they live. That it is only by change in the ownership of economic forces that any change in the condition of the people can come about—or by revolution guided by intelligence.

Parliament is the Mecca for Mastererdonic Moochers on the Make; and a *Rendezvous* for the Rich, where they exchange their opinions, and keep their interests in their own hands, or let them out at good interest.

The poor believe Parliament is a "Royal Exchange," where they can exchange bad laws for good laws: poverty for peace and plenty: and misery for happiness. We find it is the Mausoleum of New Thought: and the Morgue for Martyrs who have struggled to reach the Millennium by that path. Experience teaches this.

Men made Parliament, not Parliament men. Politics were invented to preserve the privileges of unscrupulous Egoists and perpetuate the slavery of Altruists and the horny-handed sons of toil as long as possible: that is until the people find out the inutility of politics to cure their economic evils. For they must know, some day, a political pill cannot cure an economic cancer. An economic disease must be combated by an economic remedy.

Practically, Parliament does not make laws, it only frames them or constructs them. Judges make laws, for the last precedent embalms a principle and assassinates the Rights of Man. As a manifestation of this fact I refer you to the Taff Vale decision, which paralyzed the Trade Union Acts, and inoculated many workers with the malady of thought.

The struggle for political power is between the Conservatives, the Liberals, and the Laborites.

The Conservatives or Tories have the land and other things.

The Liberals have money and other things.

The Laborites have nothing except ambition and a strong desire to get other things. The Conservatives and Liberals control everything worth having, because they have property. All power emanates from the possession of property. This is the reason the Laborites are powerless today—because they have no property. The Conservative Party consists of the Peerage, the Beerage, the Intellectual Steerage—and Arthur J. Nancy Balfour. The Liberal Party consists of the Financiers, the Middle Class Unemployed looking for work under Government, the Nonconformist Conscience, Winston Churchill—and John Burns.

The Labor Party consists of an accidental and fortuitous concourse of atoms—mostly unconscious of themselves. I classify them thusly: Political Policy-pushers with pen-pushing proclivities, Ghoul from the gutter on the growl, Altruized Egos with a yearning for a full stomach three times a day, Labor Church Devotees, Hinky-Dink Politicians, Sinners with a future and Saints with a past, She-men in knickerbockers and He-women in bloomers, Professional Sobbists and Municipal Yearnists, Mrs. Pankhurst and family,—and that Mogul of the Moanists—Keir Hardie.

These are forces arrayed against each other in the political arena.

The "Haves" will rule as long as they hold property, for power in this world has always presided where property resided. The "Have Nots" must hasten an economic evolution before they can expect a political revolution.

The Labor Party must educate their masters and pastors by bringing them disasters, for wisdom comes through sorrow and pain. As pain precedes progress, so progress must be the outcome of wisdom and wickedness or—revolution and reconstruction.

Capital is brother-in-law to the House of Lords. The House

of Lords is the stepfather of "Mars." Both are next-door neighbors and next-of-kin to Church and State, the twin-enemies of the people.

Capital is King Absolute at St. Stephens. King Edward VII reigns only at St. James's, for he is not allowed a seat in the Cabinet. He is Ruler of the Social Realm. Capital is the Ruler of the Universe.

Modern aggression is commercial, not military, with 10 per cent. as the incentive.

The House of Commons, the handmaiden of the House of Lords, a philosophic standpoint. It has no Chairman, but is more orderly than the "Commons." There are no "scenes" there, because there is more liberty for the individual. Each peer perseveres to preserve his privileges without terrible tongue-duels, wrathful riots, or Girls in the Gallery.[248]

The House of Commons is the hand-maiden of the House of Lords. Capital rules the Cabinet; the Cabinet rules the House of Commons; the House of Commons can't bear the voice of the people—and still the people believe in the gods of their forefathers. They are governed by the tomb. The dead hand of the past paralyses the brain of the present. The moral of this problem is: the people must not put their trust in politics nor Parliament, but must trust themselves before they can be free.

—THE MAN WITHOUT A SOUL.

---

248   Dora Marsden disrupted a speech by Winston Churchill as a "girl in the gallery" suffragette. Women's Rights were too limiting for her and she moved on to Egoism, founding the periodical *The Egoist*.

A Napoleon of Labor

Wanted! to lead the Reform forces of today. Must be possessed of psychic insight and brutality—of wisdom to know and brutality to do. A man who is not afraid to break the Sabbath, the Ten Commandments, or anything else he can lay his hands on; a sort of Bovrilised Brutus—or Bloodthirsty Buddha—with a head to contrive, a tongue to persuade, and a hand to execute any mischief. He must possess the audacity of Chamberlain, the verbosity of Gladstone, the wisdom of Disraeli, the persistence of Keir Hardie, the enthusiasm of Bilatchford, the wit of Bernard Shaw, the lungs of John Burns, the vivacity of Tom Mann, the insight of Machiavelli,[249] the strength of Sandow,[250] the analysis of Thomas Paine, the eloquences of Ingersoll,[251] the thoroughness of Bradlaugh,[252] the magnetism of John B. Gough, and the brutality of Malfew Seklew.— Applicants (with or without testimonials), possessing these qualities, may interview The Undersigned at this office, any day while the staff are at prayers.

—A Brutalitarian Truthist.

---

249 Niccolò di Bernardo dei Machiavelli (1469 - 1527). Author, *The Prince* (1513).
250 Eugen Sandow (1867 - 1925). Father of bodybuilding.
251 Robert Ingersoll (1833 - 1899). Agnostic orator.
252 Charles Bradlaugh (1833-1891). Member of British Parliament, Atheist, Secularist.

The Wit, Wisdom and Wickedness of Malfew Seklew

Jester-Philosopher, Founder of the Society of Superites, and President of the Society of Social Aristocrats and Conscious Egoists of England:

"Egoism is a discovery of a fact in nature, not an invention of man. It is the gospel of Common sense, the evangel of Reason, the philosophy of the 'I,' the catholicon of Self-consciousness; the theory that self-interest rules the world, not love, nor morality."

"The Conscious Egoist is a social aristocrat governed by a Master-Morality."

"A Socialist is a semi-conscious Ego dominated by a State-made morality.'

"Egoism is the apogee of intelligence, crystallized into self-knowledge."

"Egoism is Economics without Emotion."

"Egoism is Everything, because Everything is Egoism."

"The Superite is a disillusioned Ego: a man without a Soul, except his individuality; without a God, except himself; without Morality, except his own; without False Patriotism; without a Conscience, but with Consciousness of Self: without Duty, but with Divinity of Desire; without delusions economical, political, social, sexual, civil, religious, or ethical; with hedonistic pro-clivities, and libertarian ideals; propagating Economics without Agony, Politics without Team, and Sociology without a Sob."

"The Superite is a new laid Ego devoid of illusions, chimerical conceptions, and heavenly hallucinations: free from love-pox, slave-pox and smallpox. He is a 'New Spirit' struggling to be free and happy."

"The Superite is devoid of cant, humbug, hypocrisy, prejudic-es, and other brain diseases: is true to himself, while still being dominated by the progressive spirit and the surplus value of his Ego."

"The Superite is the first manifestation of Supermanism, a Su-perman in the Crude"

"The Altruist is a professional Sobbist, a mawkish Moanist on the moan, a Puritan on the prowl, a Sentimentalist suffering from emotional diarrhea."

"Altruism is a brain disease and the enemy of the Superman and the law of Progressive Life and Evolution."

"Self-knowledge is the lever that will emancipate the wage-slave, extirpate the parasite, and produce the Superman. The philoso-phy of Egoism is all that is sane in ethical, political, anarchistic, socialistic thought, culled from the writing of Nietzsche, Stirner, Brandes, Ibsen, Benj. R. Tucker, Ragnar Redbeard, George Ber-nard Shaw, Stendahl, Montaigne, Machiavelli, La Rouchefon-cauld. Emerson, Thoreau, Mandeville, Tak Kak, and *The Gospel According to Malfew Seklew.*"

"Christian morality is a morality for cheap organisms."

"Society is founded upon the patience of wage-slaves."

"Consciousness is the vivisection of the senses."

"Conscience is a cold storage warehouse, where one keeps one's prejudices—oft-times called principles, and other delusions, free of charge."

"Conscience is a torture chamber, invented by the dead to torment the living."

"Man may misunderstand Egoism, but never Egoism man."

"There are two kinds of power, economic wealth and knowledge. The poor lacking wealth must have wisdom before they have power."

"All liberties, political, civil, social, economic, sexual, religious, are valueless without economic freedom. They are dreams that pass in the night and can't be found in the day-time."

"The Missing Link in Progress, the Self-Conscious Egoist."

"The Riddle of the Ego—of the Universe, has been solved by the Superat—he has found himself Out and In."

"Can a man be a Christian, on $1 a week? He can't be anything else."

"The New Golden Rule is: Rule yourself."

"Do unto others as you would do unto yourself, if you seek self-satisfaction: if you desire reciprocity with reason."

"Man is a development from a Primordial Atomic Globule to a Glorious Globule of Gladness, from matter unconscious of itself to mind conscious of itself: from Matter to Man, from Man to Mind."

"Mind is mighty and will prevail."

"Exploitation is the First Law of Industrial and Individual Progress."

"Self Realization is the First Law of Human Nature—not Self-Preservation."

"Man is a Masterpiece of Matter, Misery and Misconception."

"Mind is a Miracle of Motion and the Marrow Fat of Matter."

"Altruism is a slave morality, invented by intellectual prostitutes to cement the structure of Superstition, Servitude, and Segregation. It is the froth of folly, the foam of faith, the fancy of fanatics, a decadent's dream, a madman's malady; the weak wild wail of weaklings, wastrels, creeplings, meeklings, christlings, and underlings, for sympathy, succour, support, and salvation."

"It is better to be a live man in a dead town than a dead man in a live town."

"Praised by these, blamed by those, I smile at fools, defy the wicked, and hasten to laugh at all, lest I be compelled to weep."

"Wise men make mistakes, but they don't repeat them."

"The man who deserves to succeed generally does."

"If you would understand the psychology of power, you must comprehend the power of personality, for the personality of power is the fulcrum of progress, and the dynamo of destiny."

"Altruism is the *delirium tremens* of thought."

"The unconscious man is an Evolutionary Process; the conscious man is an Evolutor."

"Napoleon said, 'The heart of a statesman should be in his head.' The exploited will never be saved till they make the brain the seat of their patriotic affections."

An Answer to a Symposium
The Eagle and The Serpent, February 1927

(1) Since an examination of history reveals that great egoists have been directly responsible for much of the progress in the world, do you think that a race of men endowed with conscious egoism would be conductive to an improved and happier civilization?

(2) Is Socialism a feeble expression of the Will to Power on the part of the weak, inferior creatures?

(3) Is war a cardinal requisite for progress?

A race of conscious egoists would produce the highest possible type of civilization. For conscious egoists—having found themselves out from within—would know how to do the right thing at the right time in the right way. Thus they would do today that very thing which would bring more profit and power tomorrow. They would be able to understands their own motives, their actions, their prejudices, and paralyze their own paralogies. Being vivisectors of vices, virtues, vanities, vibrations, and the eternal verities—selfishness, vanity, hate and love—they would understand themselves and human nature so well that, out of sheer enlightened selfishness, they would compel themselves to do that which would conduce to the greatest possible good to themselves and others of their kind. (2) Socialism is not a feeble expression of the Will to Power; it is merely and outburst of "socialized" agony on the part of inferior organisms, who blindly seek salvation in the wrong way. (3) War is a creator of progress, for it purifies the blood, thoughts, and brains of men. Man has been a fighting animal a million years, and because of this he is still alive and flourishing. He would otherwise have been extinct as a species a thousand years ago. War produces the Will to Power man, who is the plus-man of the period—the creator of new ideas, new conditions, new epochs. War is a good thing for posterity. A returned warrior is worth ten stay-at-home men. Fighting men are a great asset in the production of a virile breed. A man who can't or won't fight is better dead—for he makes good manure, at least... May you and the animals prosper.

With kindest regards, F. M. Wilkesbarr.

Individualism and Socialism:
A Contrast
The Eagle and The Serpent, February, 1927

Capitalism is creative.

Socialism would be co-operative.

Capitalism is aristocratic.

Socialism would be mobocratic.

Capitalism is scientific.

Socialism would be sciolistic.

Capitalism is reinforced by reason.

Socialism would be trammeled by treason.

Capitalism is explorative, exploitive, progressive.

Socialism would be expropriative, explosive, retrogressive.

Capitalism aims to give liberty to all, to make the State a servant to mankind.

Socialism would make all free by making us slaves to the State.

The Capitalist has developed organization to a science.

The Socialist has made talking a science.

The Capitalist is the creator of circumstance.

The Socialist is the creature of circumstances.

The Capitalist wears a clean collar, smiles with success.

The Socialist is Class-Conscious, a miniature Niagara of noise.

The Capitalist manipulates the present to fructify the future.

The Socialist wears a soiled collar, sneers with self-pity.

The Capitalist loves his best friends, hates his worst enemies.

The Socialist wallows in the past, fulminates in the present, and yearns for the future.

The Capitalist is opulent with optimism, rich in reason, wealthy in wisdom.

The Socialist hates his best friends (the Capitalists), loves himself without self-understanding.

The future of Capitalism lies in the present.

The Socialist is opulent with pessimism, rich in rancor, wealthy with riotous wrath.

The future of Socialism lies in the past.

Ernest Pack and John W. Gott: Malfew Seklew

The Trial and Imprisonment of J. W. Gott for Blasphemy
(excerpt). Bradford: Freethought Socialist League 1911.

Malfew Seklew, jester philosopher, was born quite early in life, and has been ahead of the times ever since. So much so, indeed, that one might with truth call him the Pilgrim of Progress and the Ishmaelite of Democracy.

Hounded out of the ranks of Demos because of his persistent propaganda of the philosophy of Egoism, he straightway conceived and founded the Society of Conscious Egoists and Social Aristocrats (the Aristocracy of brains, of course). For this daring and original step he was left alone (like all great men) to chew the cud of his psychic inspiration and find another outlet for his cardiac affinity for Demos.

When next he stoops from his lofty aristocratic pedestal it is as the Napoleon of Labour, brutally (yet withal yearningly) pointing out to the weary wage slave the pathway to salvation.

Many and brilliant have been the inspirations of this "Man without a Soul" for the emancipation of the working classes, whom he loveth while he chasteneth.

His latest emanation—up to date—is the S.I.B.-R.I.P. Policy—when in doubt or discontent "stay in bed" and "rest in peace," and the problem will solve itself. He maintains, and with some grounds, that, if all workers went on strike and stayed in bed till their demands were conceded, the economic problem (which drives so many socialists insane) would be solved, and we should enter upon an era of the most peaceful chaos the world has ever known.

So much then for the philosophy of this Iconoclast. Now for the man behind it all.

Of him it will be said, "Take him for all in all, we shall never look upon his like again." He stands alone, unique in his buoyancy and flamboyancy, the living link between Demos and the Superman.

Educated in the University of Adversity, he is—to quote himself—"a jocular jawsmith by inclination; an uncommercial traveller by occupation; and a Napoleon of Labour by inspiration." An aura of joviality pervades his personality, and he is ever ready to "down tools" and discuss the problems of the day with friend or foe. One of his favorite phrases is that he knows "more about reforming the world than any man his size and weight in the business."

In debates and discussions he is a host in himself, slaughtering his opponents mercilessly and brutally, often causing them in their agony to insult him so much that, out of sheer exuberance of his enjoyment of victory, he treats them, thus pouring oil upon the troubled waters and gaining for himself many friends.

For a quarter of a century he has been known as a Freelance and Pioneer of Progress, and has fought many battles for the right of free speech. In London, Nottingham, Newcastle and West Hartlepool he has fought against oppression and the tyranny of laws framed decades ago. Never a silent sufferer, he made a stir when the myrmidons of law and order interfered with his freedom, and he did a great deal towards showing people under what stupid legislation we are oppressed. With the weapon of ridicule he smashed the ancient laws—but we still have good men and true imprisoned for blasphemy against a being who may or may not exist. 'Tis a point of legality which wants illuminating!

But to digress no further we return to the subject of this sketch, who describes himself thus:—"I am an iconoclastic, atheistic, anarchistic, hedonistic individualist with the social instinct well developed, and with syndicalist solutions for the problem of poverty." There, in a sentence, we have the man, his philosophy and his style. Versatile and virile he amuses himself and others with his "wit, wisdom and wickedness."

Out of all this versatility, however, we select one star more brilliant than the rest. It is the Star of Criticism. As a critic of Mis(s) Messiahs of the Masses, annihilator of altruism, and vivisector of man, he shines, sparkles and scintillates, his *Labour Leader* and *Halo's Hoodoo'd* series being masterpieces of their kind.

But time presses and space compresses, so I shall conclude at once by quoting a few virile passages and epigrams from the brain of this "Smighty Atom."

"Society is an orgasm, not an organism."

"Exploitation is the first law of industrial progress."

"Idleness is the mother of invention, and the father of easy times."

"Altruistic Socialism is a brain disease; Democracy a delusion; and Christianity a cancer on the conscience of humanity."

"Politics is piffle; the ballot a bauble; Parliament a bubble; and the bible bunkum."

"Syndicalism will save sinners sooner than Christianity. It is the only way to salvation for the wage slave."

"Hunger is the great thought incubator."

"Production for profit is not the cause of poverty, but monopoly of Natural resources."

"Evolution is retail revolution; revolution is wholesale evolution."

"Man is not a religious animal; man is a selfish animal and all religions have their rewards."

Worlds Remade While You Wait
—On the East Side
New York Tribune 26 January 1919.

Zynda, Dora and Esther keep a restaurant. Zyn, Dor, Est spell Zyndorest[253]—that's what they call it. It is the only place in New York where you can eat real knishes, a delicacy made of liver, onions and raw potatoes.

When you move from the shadow of the Third Avenue "L" across the avenue to 115 East Tenth Street you can smell the redolent compounds of this Yiddish tidbit penetrating through the closed doors of Zyndorest to the damp street outside.

If it allures you and you follow it up six brownstone steps and into the first floor front you will smell the other smells— the rich smell of garlic, and the suffocation smell of blue tobacco smoke, and the smell of sweat and cheap perfume.

You will hear the babel of many tongues, the sound of spitting, purring Russian, Yiddish in all its fifty-seven varieties, and the soft gliding syllables of pidgin English, and over all the deep boom of the Sirfessor telling the world of his philosophy. He has come from Chicago via England and says he is a friend of Bernard Shaw.

And then you will relax into a long, low, running divan, and lean your elbows on a rickety table. You will not notice the fresco of violent green and yellow mattress ticking that is behind you, but your eyes will travel to the opposite side of the room from the peacock blue curtain on the window across the flyspecked door to the wall where the pictures are. It is a perpetual exhibition. Sometimes—not often—it changes; the pictures are for sale.

There is the portrait of a negress, an angry negress with an

---

253   A Jewish bohemian restaurant at 115 E. 10 Street (between 2nd and 3rd Avenues), New York City.

elongated neck and a necklace of conch-shells, holding a basket of tired-looking fruit; there is the picture of three strange trees with scarlet trunks and the picture of the writing snake with a butterfly dancing on its tail; and other pictures, painted by Rotstein and Brodowsky. At the further end of the room is the enameled door splattered with bright colors in neo-impressionistic design, by Leon Arnskey, and the door that leads to the kitchen, hung in coal-black hangings cut in an openwork design, where chinks of light peer through.

And then you feel something gentle and Slavic and soft standing beside you—it is Dora—and you hear your own voice saying, "I'll have some marinated herring," and then the babel assumes component parts. It rises up and smites you in the ear.

You are at a table with Sam, the artist; he is drawing your picture on a plate, in India ink. It's indelible, too. There's an intellectual Chinaman, he is an anarchist; a Yiddish tailor (he is eating the knishes) and the editor of a paper called *Freedom*— he expects it to be suppressed next issue. There is a fat man in a Prince Albert and checkered trousers, and a pretty little thing from uptown.

"Tell me," said the pretty little thing, leaning across the table to the tailor, "do you believe in woman suffrage?"

"Before you answer that," said the Sirfessor, "let me expound a few of the laws of Nature to you."

And the Sirfessor said: "Personality is the producer of progress, for where personality presides power resides. Next, exploitation is the first law of progress. Next, self-preservation is the first law of the ego, self-preservation is the second law of human Nature. Now, what have you got to say, my man?"

The tailor scratched his head and answered, with some thought, "I belief in wimmen's suffering."

But you turn to the expounder of the laws of Nature and ask him to expound himself and he tells you:

I am a Sirfessor. A Sirfessor is a Knight of Knowledge among benighted bipeds, peddling pestiferous piffle. I'm an Englishman by birth and a human being by adoption. I don't support myself. I live by my wits. I'm the evangelist of *The Gospel According to Malfew Seklew*, an English philosopher, called by the *Lancashire Chronicle*—that's the people's paper—the Laughing Philosopher of Lancashire. He preaches the coming of the Supercrat and the superman. There are seven stages; let me explain.

The first stage is the Simpoleon. The Simpoleon is a mass of matter that doesn't matter—except when exploited.

The second stage is the Hopeoleon. The Hopeoleon is one who suffers from inflammation of the imagination.

The third state is the Demoleon. The Demoleon is an ego on the half-shell, and he suffers from perspiration of inspiration—a semi-developed, semi-sane and hemi-hatched organism, an underdone ego with hard-boiled beliefs and cross-eyed convictions.

The fourth stage is the Psycholeon. He stands on the threshold of thought, gazing into the eyeball of ecstasy and eternity, so to speak, without getting dizzy.

The fifth stage is the Egocrat, one who has become a self-conscious egoist and recognizes that psychology precedes all progress and that enlightened egoism will make for the higher life.

The sixth stage is the Supercrat. He is first cousin to the superman-to-be. He is one who understands the seven wonders of the ego and the six hundred laws of

Nature. All Supercrats seek danger because they seek
new sensations. New sensations develop wisdom, and
wisdom is the mother of wit and wickedness.

The seventh and last stage is the Social Aristocrat. The
social aristocrat is one who has developed his social
instinct until he is able to socialize his selfishness.
The surplus value of his ego he gives away because
it increases his happiness. In doing this the sum of
happiness is increased in his environment, and the
reign of the revaluation has begun. Supermanity is here.

"Supervisor of vot?" the tailor wanted to know. "Guaranteed
by vot system?"

"The system of logic," said the Sirfessor.

"For vy don't you make a calendar of it und sell it?" began
the tailor.

The editor of *Freedom*, the new magazine, spoke suddenly
from another table. "I should be ashamed to edit any sort of
paper that wouldn't be suppressed," said he. "Read this!" and he
handed a mussed journal to the Sirfessor, who read:

Freedom, a revolutionary journal dedicated to human
freedom.

Freedom enters upon the revolutionary field as the only
English-speaking anarchist publication of the Western
Hemisphere. For its appearance we offer no apology;
we are oppressed, depressed and suppressed—yet
we carry our colors majestically amid the turbulent
conditions of Law and Order.

For many years America has been void of a publication
whose voice spoke revolution in every column. So it
is to occupy this vacant space upon the intellectual
rostrum that *Freedom* doth appear.

Its voice will shatter the foundation stones upon which human society now stands.

It advocates Destruction!

It advocates Construction!

Freedom's mission is not to patch up a worn-out system along reform, or Socialist, lines, but to abolish all existing institutions.

Revolution means Revolution—not reform.

It is only when Gods, Governments, Hypocrisy, Tyranny and Slavery crumble away into oblivion that man will be able to assert himself. Man, know thyself! Assert your individuality! Demand—work—for individual freedom.

—A. T.

"I couldn't gif five cents for dot." This was the tailor's opinion.

"An anarchist," amended the Sirfessor, "is the meekest organism that ever dashed through space backward." A young lieutenant in the uniform of the Canadian Cavalry came in at this point and stood staring at the Sirfessor, who got up and, supporting himself against the table in a lachrymose manner, continued: "Communism is the wild, weak wail of weaklings, cheaplings, meeklings and groundlings for succor, support and sympathy. Socialism is a moan in monotone for mercy and the millennium.

"Wow!" said the lieutenant.

"As I was saying," said the Sirfessor to the lieutenant, "wishes control the lives of cheap organisms; desire is intensive intensified organisms. Will is the director of destiny and the creator of the future as expressed through the notion of the will to power—man. The will to power is the elbow grease of evolution, and the engineer to progress. I am the President of the Society of Social Aristocrats. Have my card... "

"Wow!" repeated the lieutenant.

And then, while someone in broken English is telling of the new religion of Abdul Baha, which has twelve basic principles (if you want to find out about it go to the temple just around the corner; they serve free lunch too), and someone else is trying to sell you a red ticket to the IWW ball on Saturday evening, January 25, at Park View Palace, on 110th Street, you suddenly realize that the nice little thing at your table is really a very nice little thing, and you start to tell her so, but along comes Esther and she says: "This is a restaurant, not a private room."

So you fumble around for your hat and slink out, and, as the door creaks behind you, you feel the warm smell of cooking following you to the street and the voice of the Sirfessor saying: "I am the only one who knows anything about the Mentoid of Mirth, new science... " and you are out in the clear night air.

—uncredited

Tom-Cat Vibrators, "Hamlets," and Ordinary "Reds"

excerpt, *Literary Digest* 17 July 1920.

Perhaps you have never heard of Trip-Hammer Johnson. There was a time when France had never heard of Napoleon, Johnson will remind you. To be sure, Trip-Hammer doesn't flash in the spotlight like Bill Haywood. He has never run for President, like Gene Debs. If you would understand the humanity-savers you must know Johnson. Radicalism numbers among its followers countless Johnsons, each dreaming of world power, but when Trip-Hammer, with his many vibrations, is the most interesting specimen of the type.

He is easily found by this who seek his wisdom. Go down State Street, in Chicago, past the "L" into the blighted district "south of Van Buren." Turn into the twenty-five-cent hotel at the corner of Congress Street. On the second floor, sprawling in somber taciturnity before a window, you will find him.

You will know him by his gigantic beetle-brow. You will know him by his huge body, by his heavy, drooping mustache, which he is forever twisting, by his dreamy blue Norsemen's eyes, by the three-deep wrinkles that furrow his forehead as he sits and cerebrates. Perhaps Johnson won't talk to you after you find him, for he may think you are a spy. Spies have followed him for twenty years, he says. And if you are so tactless as to interrupt him in one of his more thoughtful moments, he will "throw vibrations" at you and drive you away.

I remember my first encounter with Johnson. I was sitting at a table in a radical "hang-out" on the North Side, drinking coffee with Sirfessor Wilkesbarre, another humanity saver. Trip-Hammer suddenly thrust his dour face into the room and seeing the Sirfessor, came to the table and challenged him to debate. Long conversation followed.

I was extolling the virtues of the IWW. Wilkesbarre had a philosophy of his own, a sort of Friedrich Nietzsche / Ragnar Redbeard jumble, which he called Supermanity. He was assailing me hotly as I dilated on industrial unionism and the creed of Haywood. Johnson was disdainfully silent; he favored me with a pitying gaze, and then leaned back in his chair emitting audible symptoms of boredom. At last, in mock seriousness, I shook my finger at my listeners.

"When the crisis comes," I demanded, "when the system crashes in confusion and chaos—if you repudiate the IWW, who is there who can step forward and take charge of the world?"

As one man they both arose.

"Supermanity will!" barked the Sirfessor.

"I will!" roared Johnson, thumping himself on the chest.

That reply is characteristic of Trip-Hammer; he is ready at all times to take charge of the world. The Sirfessors may trust in philosophies to save humanity, but Trip-Hammer knows that humanity can only saved only by Trip-Hammer.

Once I attempted to flatter Johnson and met with disaster. He had been boring me for two hours, dilating upon Havelock Ellis and Krafft-Ebbing. Suddenly I burst out in mock enthusiasm.

"Johnson! You are one of the greatest scientist in the world... "

"Stop!" Johnson's voice rang out venomously as he pointed his finger rebukingly at me.

"'One of the greatest'—rot!" he bellowed. "I am the greatest!"

Of course, to such an announcement I could make no reply.

He pulled a sheaf of well-thumbed greasy papers from his pockets and shook them at me belligerently.

"Let you IWW coyotes beat that!" he boasted. His voice dropped confidentially.

"I am the mastermind of the revolution. In these papers lie

the secret of perpetual motion! Discovered by me! I have merely to act and the world is in my hands. I'll show you! 'One of the best,' huh? Wait till Johnson's trip-hammer falls!"

In 1917, when the first victories of Bolshevism burst into the news, a wave of excitement ran through the radical groups. I was in Chicago and I remember the goings-on in the Socialist and IWW national offices. There was a wild scramble of egos. There were hot struggles between personalities, each seeking to overshadow the other. All felt that it was now or never. For was not Bolshevism coming? Who was to be the future Lenin, the destined Trotsky? Each felt the call of greatness.

There was one great man who bellowed to the crowd at headquarters: "I am ready! Robspierre slumbers in my bosom." Another began to read the life of Jean Paul Marat. Little Louis Fraina startled everybody by growing a beard *a la* Trotsky. Bill Hayward began to wear Gladstone collars. John Reed[254] affected proletarian garb and howled like a Comanche. All the while, in the background, sat Trip-Hammer Johnson, watching with cold, scornful eyes, chuckling ironically from time to time, wallowing in the delirious thought which he whispered sometimes to those he trusted:

"Let them all rave! They'll have to come to me in the end— when Johnson begins to throw vibrations."

I sometimes wonder if Trip-Hammer was not the sanest of them all.

—uncredited

---

254   John Reed (1887 - 1920). Journalist, witness to Bolshevik Revolution.

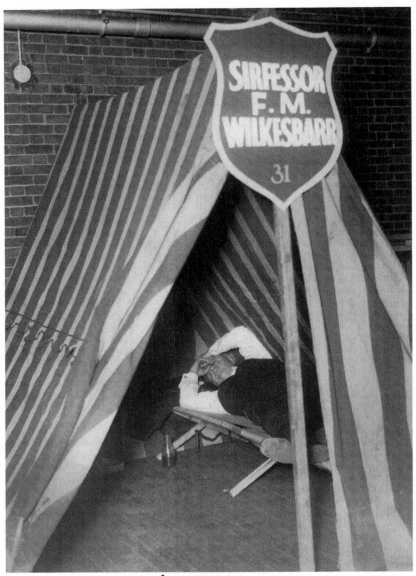

100114

TALKED HIMSELF OUT OF THE TALKING MARATHON
Sirfesser F.M. Wilkesbarre, one of the entrants in the
World's Championship Gab Fest being held in New York
City, taking things easy sleeping and resting his vocal
cords after dropping out of the race. The Sirfessor
declared he did not have his heart in the work, and
with one last gutteral gurgle he turned over and went
to sleep.

YOUR CREDIT LINE MUST READ (ACME)

Noun and Verb Rodeo[255]

Runs Out of Words, Put Out of Contest

The championship "noun and verb rodeo" at the Seventy-First Regiment Armory ended its twenty-four hours yesterday afternoon with the loss of only one contestant. [...] Professorial and fully determined to win, is Sirfessor F. M. Wilkesbarr, S.S.M.M. Lord of Interpretations, Master of Mentoidology, and the demigod of the demi-damned. "Coiner of more new words than any man in the world" and manufacturer of epigrams "transcending the wit of Shakespeare," the Sirfessor is a reticent but honest man.

—New York City, New York: *New York Times* 27 December 1928.

Seven Quit Talking Match

Among those who dropped out during the day were "Sirfessor" Wilkesbarr, Mme. Anet Berrie, actress; Miss May Shaw, Bible reader; Di Gurco, a singing Italian, Simon Long, Jean Cabell O'Neill, who was forced out by the doctor's orders, and Captain Smoke Risley.

—New York City, New York: *New York Times* 28 December 1928.

---

255   In the time of "dance marathon" publicity stunts, one man decided his own spin would be a "talking marathon," beginning Christmas Eve of 1928. The Sirfessor took part, and for this gained one of his few national media references. This story might have found a place nearer the front of the book had he actually won.

Malfew Seklew Solves
All Problems of Life

Sirfessor Wilkesbarre Will Lecture

Sirfessor Wilkesbarre lectures Society of Social Aristocrats,
"From Simpoleon to Superman," Sun., 8pm, 613 Masonic Temple.

—Chicago, Illinois: *The Day Book* 29 January 1916.

Sirfessor Wilkesbarre Will Lecture

Sirfessor Wilkesbarre will lecture on "Altruism, an Enemy of
the People," before Society Social Aristocrats, Colonial Hall,
20 W. Randolph, Sun. 8 pm.

—Chicago, Illinois: *The Day Book* 12 February 1916.

Society of Social Aristocrats

Society of Social Aristocrats, Colonial Hall, 20 W. Randolph,
Sirfessor Wilkesbarre speaks: "Socialism a Brain Disease."

—Chicago, Illinois: *The Day Book* 19 February 1916.

Sirfessor Wilkesbarre's Class

Sirfessor Wilkesbarre's class, Sat. 8 pm. Worker's Inst., 920 S. Ashland.

—Chicago, Illinois: *The Day Book* 24 February 1916.

Sirfessor Wilkesbarre and B. Lester Weber

Sirfessor Wilkesbarre and B. Lester Weber will debate before
Society of Social Aristocrats. Colonial Hall, 20 W. Randolph,
8 pm, Sun.

—Chicago, Illinois: *The Day Book* 26 February 1916.

Sirfessor Wilkesbarre

Sirfessor Wilkesbarre will open class on how to be a superman, and the evolution of the ego. 8 pm Sat., Workers' Inst., 920 S. Ashland.

—Chicago, Illinois: *The Day Book* 2 March 1916.

Sirfessor Wilkesbarre Lectures

Sirfessor Wilkesbarre lectures. Colonial Hall, 20 W. Randolph, 8 pm, Sun. "The Super-socialism."

—Chicago, Illinois: *The Day Book* 4 March 1916.

Sirfessor Wilkesbarre Will Start Class

Sirfessor Wilkesbarre will start class for study of supermanism, for men and women. 8 pm, Workers Inst., 920 S. Ashland av.

—Chicago, Illinois: *The Day Book* 7 March 1916.

Sirfessor Wilkesbarre Will Lecture

Sirfessor Wilkesbarre will lecture for the Workers' inst., at West Side Auditorium, Taylor and Racine av., 8 pm, Fri.: "Can Socialism Save the People." D. Mehlmon will lecture: "Stirner and Nietzsche," Radical Library, 712 S. Loomis, 8pm, Sat.

—Chicago, Illinois: *The Day Book* 9 March 1916.

Class and Debate

Class for students of "The Seven Wonders of the Ego," Workers Inst., 920 S. Ashland av. 8pm tonight, Sirfessor Wilkesbarre. Debate: "Egoism vs. Socialism." Colonial Hall, 20 W. Randolph, 8 pm, Sun. Sirfessor F. M. Wilkesbarre and M. Ritman.

—Chicago, Illinois: *The Day Book* 11 March 1916.

Seven Wonders and Debate

Sirfessor Wilkesbarre speaks to his class at Workers Inst., 920 S. Ashland av. 8pm tonight on "The Seven Wonders of the Ego."

"Is There a Creator?" Debate with W. C. Bohanna, affirmative; Sirfessor Wilkesbarre, negative. Colonial Hall, 20 W. Randolph, 8 pm, Sun.

—Chicago, Illinois: *The Day Book* 17 March 1916.

Debate and Meet

Debate: "Altruism is a Fundamental Principle of Nature." Affirmative, G. G. Florine; negative, Sirfessor Wilkesbarre. 20 W. Randolph, Sun. 8 pm. Independent Society of Aristocrats meets Sun. 8 pm 128 W. Randolph. Symposium of speakers in charge of Sirfessors Sullivan, Anderson and Norman.

—Chicago, Illinois: *The Day Book* 1 April 1916.

Debate

Debate: "Karl Marx vs. Malfew Seklew; Which is the Better System of Philosophy?" Moses Baritz and Sirfessor Wilkesbarre, 20 W. Randolph, Sun. 8 pm., auspices Society of Social Aristocrats and Supercrats.

—Chicago, Illinois: *The Day Book* 8 April 1916.

Society of Superites and Supercrats

Society of Superites and Supercrats meets at Colonial Hall, 20 W. Randolph, Sun 8 pm. Debate: "Is Socialism Desirable?" Affirmative: Jack Carney, late of Irish rebel army. Negative: F. M. Wilkesbarre, Sirfessor of Superology.

—Chicago, Illinois: *The Day Book* 25 November 1916.

Debate

Debate, Sun. 8 pm, Colonial Hall, 20 W. Randolph. "Resolved: That Malfew Seklew Solves All Problems of Life." Affirmative: Sirfessor Wilkesbarre. Negative: John Loughman. M. C. Walsh, chairman.

—Chicago, Illinois: *The Day Book* 1 December 1916.

Debate

Debate: "Socialism." Colonial Hall, 20 W. Randolph. Sun., 7:45 pm. Affirmative: John T. Vaughan. Negative: Sirfessor Wilkesbarre.

> —Chicago, Illinois: *The Day Book* 1 December 1916.

Debate

John Loughman and Sirfessor Wilkesbarre will debate before Society of Superites at Colonial Hall, 20 W. Randolph, Sun., Jan 7, 8 pm. Subject: "Resolved, That Ignorance is More Beneficial to the Race than Knowledge."

> —Chicago, Illinois: *The Day Book* 2 January 1917.

Debate

Society of Superites, Colonial Hall, 8 pm. Debate, Sirfessor Wilkesbarre and John Loughman: "Resolved, That Ignorance is More Beneficial to the Race than Knowledge."

> —Chicago, Illinois: *The Day Book* 6 January 1917.

Sirfessor Wilkesbarre Will Speak

Sirfessor Wilkesbarre will speak on "Birth Control" at Colonial Hall, 110 W. Randolph, Sun eve., 8 pm.

> —Chicago, Illinois: *The Day Book* 13 January 1917.

Sirfessor Wilkesbarre Lectures

Sirfessor Wilkesbarre lectures on *The Ego and His Own* at Hobo College, 917 W. Washington Blvd., 8 pm.

> —Chicago, Illinois: *The Day Book* 12 April 1917.

Today on the Radio

WGBS 5:45 The Sirfessor Speaks.

> —New York City, New York: *New York Times* 4 July 1931.

OBITS

Forty Years on a Soap Box

In a tiny apartment on the top floor in a rear tenement east of Sturyvesant Square, the Sirfessor shares a menage with Dan O'Brien, the King of the Hobos. Mr. O'Brien was not present, being in Washington when this department visited the establishment and listened to the Sirfessor expounding his views.

A stout, white-haired, cheerful, rubinsund Yorkshireman of some seventy years, F. M. Wilkesbarr has enjoyed an extraordinary career. For forty years he has gone up and down the face of the earth, untroubled by ambition, sometimes well-to-do, at others living, as he says, "by my wits." He started a half century ago as a herb doctor in Nottingham. He was for a time part owner of a prosperous business in Manchester. [...]

He was one of the first to bang the big drum for Nietzsche at a time when *Thus Spake Zarathustra* was the only work of the German's translated into English. In his time he has swallowed and preached nationalism, atheism, socialism, communism, anarchism, all of which he now dismisses with a smile as childish fancies.

His prophet now is Malfew Seklew, concerning whose identity and mysterious name he was able to give this department very little information though he lent me Seklew's magnum opus...

The Sirfessor, it turned out, is not entirely without ambition. He would like to live until he has completed the revision of his book *Forty Years of Soap-Boxing*. After which, he says, he will have no further interest in life...

—New York City, New York: *New York Evening Post* 15 April 1930.

Soap-Box King, 77, Dies in Bellevue

Fred M. Wilkes, who peddles ideologies and panaceas to the masses in the chief soap-box forums of the world, died yesterday afternoon of a pulmonary disease in Bellevue Hospital. In his seventy-seventh year, he had yet to find a personal millennium, for his friends were trying last night to save him from a pauper's grave...

In his days of comparative well-being, when he discoursed on the distribution of property, Wilkes bulked 240 pounds. But last Friday, when he was taken to the hospital, he had shrunk to 100.

The home and "study" of the orator was a four-room flat at 344 First Avenue. The building had been abandoned and had been condemned by the city in 1934, but Wilkes took possession, invoking the doctrine of squatters' rights, and paying no rent. His recent income was an old-age pension.

A reported called yesterday at the old dwelling and, surprisingly enough, the doorbell worked and a man about 50 years old answered. It developed that he was Wilke's Boswell, busy gathering up piles of notes left in the apartment by his intellectual master. Insisting on semi-anonymity, the man said he was "Potter."

—New York City, New York: *New York Times* 10 February 1938.

The Gospel According to Malfew Seklew

Superite Tie-Frame

"His specialty was a tie-frame, a handy little article the use of which he was one of the first to demonstrate in the market-places of this country. His manner of selling the tie-frame was quite original.

After showing how the thing was to be fitted on to the collar, he proceeded to embellish his demonstration in amusing phraseology. 'You place it through the clip in this manner, allowing the end to repose placidly upon the palpitating bosom. Should you be suffering with a cold on the chest, it is as good as a mustard plaster. Should you, on the other hand, be troubled by a cold in the head, you can pick it up and blow your nose with it. Each tie is guaranteed to last for forty years. If, at the end of forty years, it is worn out, bring it back here and your money will be returned.'"

—from *Hyde Park Orator* (1934) by Bonar Thompson

◄ *Advertisement from the pamphlet* The Gospel According to Malfew Seklew.

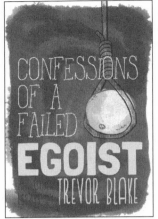

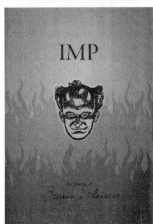

Made in the USA
Middletown, DE
16 September 2021

48467712R00168